ACTING SHAKESPEARE

ACTING SHAKESPEARE

JOHN GIELGUD

WITH JOHN MILLER

Acting Shakespeare by John Gielgud with John Miller

ISBN 1-55783-374-5

The material which appears in Appendix II was originally published as anIntroduction to Rosamund Gilder's book on John Gielgud as Hamlet in America

Library of Congress Cataloging-in-Publication Data

Library of Congress Catalog Card Number: 99-64646

APPLAUSE BOOKS

211 West 71st Street
New York, NY 10023
Phone (212) 496-7511
Fax: (212) 721-2856

10 9 8 7 6 5 4 3 2

PRINTED IN CANADA

To Peter Brook
with gratitude, affection and admiration

CONTENTS

ACKNOWLEDGEMENTS

Many of the illustrations come from Sir John Gielgud's own collection; those on pages 2, 4, 5, 6, 7, 8, 9, 10 bottom, 12 bottom, 13, 14, 16, 20 top, 21, 25 top, 26 bottom were supplied by The Theatre Museum, by courtesy of the Board of Trustees of the Victoria and Albert Museum. The photographs on pages 18, 19, 20 bottom, 22 top left and right, 23, 26 top, 27 were reproduced by permission of the Angus McBean Estate; those on pages 13 top left, 17, 37, 38 and 40 by the John Vickers Theatre Collection; on pages 1, 29 bottom, 30 and 31 by Marc Guillaumot; 29 top and 32 by Pief Weyman; and on page 24 by Janus Productions Limited.

The Reviews in Appendix I are reproduced with thanks to the *Sunday Times* for James Agate's reviews of *Romeo and Juliet* and *Hamlet*; to the *Observer* for Ivor Brown's review of *Romeo and Juliet*, and Robert Cushman's of *The Tempest*; to the *Daily Telegraph* for W.A. Darlington's review of *Romeo and Juliet*; to the *Illustrated London News* for J.C. Trewin's review of *The Tempest*; and to *The Times* for reviews of *Hamlet, Richard II, Lear* and *The Tempest*.

The authors are also indebted to Wally Plummer, Barry Norman, Charles McDonald, and Jill Young for particular help in several stages of preparation of this book; and to Ingrid Connell, Kit Coppard, Hilary Engel and Richard Milner at Sidgwick and Jackson for their work on its production.

To JOHN MILLER

(not to be confused with JONATHAN of the same name)

Dear John

Although I was very happy collaborating with you in 1979 on *An Actor and His Time*, it has taken you several months of patient coaxing to persuade me to put my hand to another collection of reminiscences – for that is what the ensuing chapters seem to have amounted to, now that I have clumsily put them together.

It was your suggestion that I should try to concentrate on my many experiences with Shakespeare, but this prospect only dismayed me further. Having been lucky enough to play many of the great parts, as well as directing a number of the best-known plays over so many years, I suppose it was natural for some people, yourself included, to credit me with being an authority on the subject. But I fear I must disappoint you. I am neither a scholar nor an intellectual, and I have naturally hesitated to trespass on so many well-trodden and controversial paths. However, I feel sure that your diligent enthusiasm will enable you to give some sort of shape to the ensuing pages in order to weld them into a readable narrative. I can only hope that I have not repeated too many of the opinions and anecdotes which I have used in various other books and interviews, and that I may still perhaps be able to contribute some slight amusement to a few stagestruck readers of the present generation without taking myself too seriously.

During the fifteen years since I moved to the country I have seldom been to the theatre or the cinema more than once or twice a year, and so cannot help feeling very much a back-seat driver, wary of making rash pronouncements about the present, and fearing to become a bore with nostalgic memories of the theatre of my youth

Good luck in your patient endeavours on my behalf.

As ever yours

John Gielgud

1991.

FOREWORD

SHAKESPEARE – HIT OR MISS?

IT IS odd that I should have been so much associated in my career with Shakespeare, because I have never been a great reader of poetry or even chosen to read it for my private pleasure. As a boy I came to like the more romantic plays. At my prep school I remember playing a scene from *The Merchant of Venice* and one from *Julius Caesar,* liking the speeches very much and learning some of them by heart. My parents took me to see Shakespeare sometimes when I was a boy, but I was chiefly attracted in those early days by the scenery and costumes and romantic atmosphere. Because of my lack of interest in politics, I have never been greatly attracted by *Coriolanus, Cymbeline,* or *Troilus and Cressida,* plays that I still know only slightly even today.

I find I have to be involved in a play in order to become absorbed by it, and I have always been somewhat ashamed never to have appreciated the work of Beckett and Brecht, since I think if I had ever acted in one of their plays I might have learned to understand them better, as I did with Shakespeare.

I came to two or three of the plays quite late in my career. I had never taken much interest in either *The Winter's Tale* or *Measure For Measure* until I had seen them performed and been attracted by the parts of Leontes and Angelo.

It was the pasteboard glitter of the theatre which most appealed to me, and which I have never ceased to love. I was especially fascinated by *Romeo and Juliet* when I first acted Romeo. But, though I was thrilled to be given the chance of playing such a famous leading part when I was only nineteen, I was inclined to blame H.K. Ayliff for my failure in it. He had been Sir Barry Jackson's principal director for some years at Birmingham, and was to me a forbidding and unapproachable personality. I was of course delighted that he had finally chosen me (after several daunting auditions) and thought his handling of the text both lively and intelligent. But he had allowed Paul Shelving (one of Jackson's favourite designers) to contrive a practical but bleak setting, and to give me a wig and costumes which were neither comfortable nor becoming. I certainly had no help from Ayliff at rehearsals, and I had to depend for help and criticism on the wonderfully generous assistance of Gwen Ffrangcon-Davies, who was my fascinating Juliet, and a wise and charming actor named Campbell Gullan, who played Friar Lawrence and told me he had never acted in Shakespeare before. He had written out his lines in modern prose in a little notebook in order to digest their precise meaning before he set out to memorise them from the text.

I had my first experience of stage fright at the opening performance. As I stood in the wings before my first entrance, I thought to myself 'What if I slipped out into the street and disappeared? Everything would be in turmoil – the audience, the company – the evening would be a complete disaster, while I would be far away, completely uninvolved.' A strange fantasy to invent at such a moment, but I have never been able to forget it.

INTRODUCTION

A Shakespearean Chronology

by John Miller

JOHN GIELGUD's professional service to Shakespeare now spans 70 years, from his one line as the English Herald in the 1921 Old Vic *Henry V* –

'Here is the number of the slaughter'd French'

– to his screen Prospero in 1991, in which he speaks almost every line in the play, a responsibility that would daunt any but the greatest actor.

His admiration for our greatest playwright goes back even further. He played Mark Antony and Shylock at school and was regularly taken to the theatre by different members of the Terry family. He still remembers as one of his most thrilling and formative experiences in the theatre being taken to the great Shakespeare Tercentenary Gala at Drury Lane in 1916, when he was just 12 years old. He knew his adored great-aunt, Ellen Terry, only at the end of her life when her memory was fading, but he was enchanted by the magical talent that had made her so famous and popular as Henry Irving's leading lady.

His intuitive feel for the verse was apparent from the beginning. When he played Romeo to Gwen Ffrangcon-Davies's Juliet in 1924 one critic, who confessed he was unacquainted with his previous achievements noted: 'He has a good presence and a musical voice, and he speaks his lines with an apparent consciousness that they are both poetry and sense.' But Ivor Brown was less impressed with his other attributes: 'Mr Gielgud's body from his hips down never meant anything throughout the evening. He has the most meaningless legs imaginable.'

In successive years he took smaller parts in *The Two Gentlemen of Verona, The Tempest, Hamlet,* and *Othello,* in which his Cassio is notable for also being the first, but far from the last, time in which the Gielgud profile was featured by the cartoonists. But it was his two seasons leading the Old Vic Company in 1929–31 that established him in the forefront of Shakespearean actors. He began with Romeo again, then Antonio in *The Merchant of Venice,* and his third rôle of Richard II set the company and the audience by the ears, and impressed the critics: '... much the best thing this talented young actor has done so far'; '... with a command of noble pose and gesture, a gracious melancholy mien, and a lovely handling of the language to which one would not refuse the highest admiration'; '... he speaks well, moves well, has a sensitive intelligence both for the rhythm and the sense of a line, and plenty of controlled and restrained vigour. He is teaching himself a lot by playing long parts at the Old Vic.' 'He spoke the verse with sense and sensibility, and negotiated the subtle transitions of mood, from exaltation to despair, without turning transpontine somersaults. This young actor is profiting visibly from his repertorial experience and grows steadily in power.'

The variety of leading roles he played at the Old Vic revealed that power in both tragedy and comedy. In *A Midsummer Night's Dream* his command of the verse gave him the key to his characterisation. As *The Times* observed: 'Mr Gielgud's Oberon knows exceptionally well how to be a monarch and a poet with a discreet tongue in his cheek and a twinkle in his eye.'

The Director at the Old Vic, Harcourt Williams, was a devotee of Harley Granville-Barker, as was Gielgud, and they always heeded their mentor's insistence on pace. In *Julius Caesar* Williams had the Crowd surging up out of the orchestra pit (an effect echoed in John Schlesinger's 1977 National Theatre production), and Gielgud's Mark Antony made his first line in the Forum a natural and hurried appeal for listeners in a tumult. The Cassius was Donald Wolfit, the part in which Gielgud 20 years later was to electrify both stage and film audiences.

When, next, he approached Macbeth, Harcourt Williams noted how Gielgud achieved the appearance of weight and age by choosing heavy cloaks from the wardrobe and wisely rehearsing in them. Williams was reminded of Irving, and thought Gielgud had inherited Ellen Terry's skill in his ability to make a cloak act. One critic thought his performance would have been remarkable in a player double his age. James Agate believed that in this play Shakespeare struck his richest vein of poetry, and was convinced that Gielgud's Macbeth had 'supped full with horrors', conveying the ravages of mind, soul and body he had endured when he re-entered after the sleep-walking scene. Intriguingly, another critic saw his motivation after the meeting with the weird sisters as 'less of the fighting Scotsman than the Dane; and indeed, all through the play Mr Gielgud is busy establishing a close relationship with Hamlet.'

He was in fact rehearsing Hamlet while he was playing Macbeth, and it was his first assumption of the former that brought new audiences flocking across the Thames to the Old Vic. Ivor Brown said: 'This performance puts him beyond the range of the arriving actors; he is in the first rank.' Agate this time went even further: 'I have no hesitation in saying that it is the high-water mark of English Shakespearean acting in our time.' Sybil Thorndike was swept right off her feet into another life 'far more real than the life I lived in, and moved, moved beyond words.'

The Times encapsulated the quality of the interpretation that prompted these responses:

> This Hamlet is noble in conception. It has been thought out in the study, and is lived upon the stage, with the result that you feel that these things are happening to Hamlet for the first time, and that he is, here and now, creating the words which shall express the new-felt emotions. The performance is not actorish and the affair of repetition; this Hamlet will cease upon, and about, the midnight with no pain, and that will be the end of him.

This final production of the season was such a success that it transferred to the West End to similar acclaim, the forerunner of several later productions of this play in which he was to star and sometimes direct as well.

For the new Old Vic season that opened in September 1930, he was joined for the first time by Ralph Richardson. On the first night of *Henry IV*, Part I, there was not even enough standing room available, and several women fainted at the back of the stalls. Hotspur's fiery speech, 'My liege, I did deny no prisoners . . .' thrilled the audience then, as it did me and the rest of the audience at his *Ages of Man* recital many years later, and still does any listener to the record he made of that virtuoso performance.

Richardson's Prince Hal to Gielgud's Hotspur began their lifelong partnership, but it was the next production that cemented it. Richardson was struggling with Caliban in rehearsal until Gielgud offered to rehearse privately the scenes with Prospero. The setting was oriental, Caliban looking like an ogre in a Japanese fairy-tale, with his hair in long strings and a tonsured head, and a face like a Mongolian devil-mask; Prospero in a turban and clean-shaven, with a long crimson mantle sweeping over his dark green robe, standing on a high lacquer-red Chinese bridge. Played young enough to be the father of a 15-year-old girl, this Prospero's voice had the weary cadence of an embittered maturity, his bearing the stateliness of a magician impatient of opposition. According to Ivor Brown:

> Here is the Italian gentleman, a decoration to any gallery, rich in Shakespeare's essential melancholy, a poet on whose music one hangs with fresh excitement and delight. He needs no wand to be a sorcerer; his magic is in his mind, as his disenchantment with the world of men is in his anguished eye and the dying fall of his declamation. I was seeing the real Prospero for the first time.

This Prospero was to work his magic on four later occasions, the last three for young directors all called Peter (Brook 1957, Hall 1974, Greenaway 1991).

The next two plays were less successful. *Antony and Cleopatra* had not been seen in a London theatre for twenty years, and it is easy to forget how much Shakespeare had been neglected in the earlier part of this century, until Gielgud revived his box-office appeal at the Old Vic and later in the West End. But Antony was not really his part. As *The Star* put it:

> Mr Gielgud is happiest with a hero who has brains or at least ideas. He has a genius for revealing the subtler thoughts of his characters. The vigorous soldier smitten with a woman gave him no chance to do this. If we were disappointed it was because the part gives him no scope for this psychological acting, but he produced some rare vigour and bombast, drank like a trooper, and made love like a hussar.

It is rare for Gielgud to go against the text, but he assumed a beard for Antony, which drew Agate's disapproval: 'Add a harp to this actor's attire and he would have made a very creditable

Wolfram; a staff and bedgown would have turned him into a friar. There is talk in the play of Antony being barber'd ten times o'er, whereas Mr Gielgud implied the desert's contempt for razors'.

Twelfth Night did not come up to Gielgud's own expectations, but he restored his faith in himself and that of others with *Much Ado About Nothing*. His delight in Benedick was to bring him huge acclaim in the Fifties, but already in 1931 he showed his command of the part. W.A. Darlington in the *Daily Telegraph* was astonished by his versatility, which was making a fascinating actor ripen into a great one: 'Nobody who had seen him only in *Hamlet* would have recognised him in the hearty young soldier and wit who wooed Beatrice last night. His Benedick is the personification of virility and spontaneous gaiety – a most attractive performance.'

Even with one reservation Agate thought he set an example other actors ought to try and emulate: 'Mr Gielgud's Benedick is a little wanting in swagger in the early scenes, in which he should be more of a Terry. But this actor does well later on, and I suggest that a professional matinée should be given, so that our young players may hear from his delivery of the "behaviour in love" soliloquy how to speak English prose with beauty, point, and audibility.' (For those who wish to take advantage of it, this opportunity now exists on record.)

His partner, as in so many of these early Old Vic productions, was Dorothy Green, and her Beatrice attracted plaudits too. And Darlington's notice was anxious not to leave out the credit due to the man who directed all of them: 'Mr Harcourt Williams continues to show himself a subtle and intriguing producer. Having so good a Benedick and Beatrice to rely on, he has taken entirely the right course in emphasising the comedy and touching in the serious scenes as lightly as may be, and is to be congratulated on an outstanding success.'

The part in which John Gielgud bade farewell to the Old Vic

in 1931 was the one in which he was to return in very different circumstances in 1940: King Lear. What struck him, in first studying it, was that even when Lear's brain has gone he retains his bodily strength. He brought this out in his performance by basing his make-up on a seventeenth-century print of Anger, as virile as a Michelangelo drawing. Vocally he did not find Lear as trying as Macbeth, where he had found the last act was a great strain.

The two seasons of playing the great tragic characters had convinced him that their creator must have been an actor, not a member of the nobility with no practical experience of the stage. In particular he was struck how the character of Lear tires as the actor himself becomes physically tired, and blessed the author for the breathing-spaces he provided in all the big parts.

The Times compared his Lear unfavourably with his previous Old Vic appearances: 'Once his imagination has been fired he is stirred to his best, and hitherto his best has sufficed. But he cannot be said to attain to the full height of Lear. It is a mountain of a part, and at the end of the evening, the peak remains unconquered.'

Agate admired the intelligence and attack of the opening:

> Mr Gielgud, lacking the physique upon which to build something patriarchal, presented a man prematurely old, a man wasting away like King John in the orchard at Swinstead Abbey. In the early scenes he touched many right notes, suggested the arrogance and the impatience, was wholly lovely in his half-listenings to the Fool, invented one superb gesture when, returning to Goneril, he veiled his face, and achieved a fine climax in the 'terrors of the earth' speech, which, in the present arrangement, concludes the first act.

Although he felt the actor was rather overwhelmed by the

elements in the storm scene, Agate recognised he was setting high standards of criticism for a man just 26, and hoped he would not feel the judgment too harsh: 'In the manifest intelligence displayed throughout and in the speaking of the verse, it is fine; time only can do the rest.'

Darlington thought he did not yet carry the guns for Lear, and the storm dominated him instead of he the storm: 'Last night at the Old Vic Mr John Gielgud made a gallant and distinguished attempt to prove that Charles Lamb was wrong when he said that *King Lear* is unactable. Mr Gielgud failed. But he failed in a manner which makes it possible to hope that some day he may succeed.' The hope was not misplaced. In two out of his next three assaults on this acting pinnacle he conquered it, and was defeated only by the additional burdens imposed by the designer in the third approach, the controversial 'Japanese *Lear*' in 1955.

Gielgud has always said that those early years at the Old Vic were the turning-point in his career. But he had also often fretted that Lilian Baylis's slender resources did not run to mounting the productions in the settings and costumes the performances deserved. His now-established crowd-pulling appeal enabled him to do Shakespeare full justice in the West End, and abroad, in the Thirties.

In 1934 he essayed Hamlet again, this time in his own production. The striking designs were by the three-woman team known collectively as Motley, who had first ravished the eye in his production for the OUDS of *Romeo and Juliet*, and who met his always exacting demands for both authenticity and pictorial beauty. The old nineteenth-century saw that 'Shakespeare spells ruin' was now happily disproved: this *Hamlet* cost about £1,500 to put on, and the production expenses were paid off in the first two weeks. When it finally ended its run at the New Theatre it had taken over £33,000, and the Gielgud record of 155 consecutive performances was the longest since Irving's in 1874.

Agate paid tribute to his speaking of the soliloquies, comparing 'O, what a rogue and peasant slave' to the first movement of some tremendous concerto, followed by 'To be, or not to be' with the tenderness of a Mozartian slow movement. He observed how the portrait had deepened in intensity:

> When Mr Gielgud played the part four years ago I suggested that while knowing when he ought to be pathetic he had not, in fact, much pathos. This has been remedied to a very remarkable degree, and the spectator must have a heart of stone not to be moved by Hamlet's obvious affection for his dead father, made manifest in the little 'Take him for all in all' colloquy with Horatio. Mr Jack Hawkins plays very well here, being staggered at Hamlet's 'Methinks I see my father', a little disappointed to find that his news is no news, and not sorry to hear that Hamlet is talking only of his mind's eye.

But Agate's exacting standards made him wish the actor had given the prose passages the same loving attention he had devoted to the poetry: 'One would then say wholeheartedly that this is Mr Gielgud's intensest fulfilment of himself, and not inquire too closely whether an Irving or a Forbes-Robertson had richer stores of magic upon which to draw. This Hamlet abounds in loveliness, but one feels that the actor's treasury could yield more.' (Ten years later Agate's hope would at last be satisfied.)

Raymond Mortimer in the *Spectator* was as attracted by the conception as by the performance:

> Mr Gielgud has swept away the obscurity of the Middle Ages and given us in a Renaissance Court a most reasonable

> and civilised Prince.... Mr Gielgud makes him an intellectual, a civilised man in an uncivilised country – or rather in a country which, like England at the end of the sixteenth century, was absorbing the manners of civilisation more rapidly than its spirit.... Altogether this is the best production of *Hamlet* which I have ever seen or am ever likely to see.

W.A. Darlington asserted that he had established himself as the first Hamlet of our time, that no actor had possessed in greater measure the special qualities that Hamlet requires, and was emboldened to state his conviction 'that there can have been few to equal him in the long history of the English stage.' The first-night audience expressed its appreciation in a slightly different form, listening throughout in a hushed silence and erupting at the end in 'a tempest of cheers' and calling the actors back for over a dozen curtain-calls.

Word of this success was quick to cross the Atlantic, and Gielgud repeated his triumph on Broadway two years later under Guthrie McClintic's direction. There on opening night the audience applauded for fifteen minutes and brought him back for sixteen curtain calls. Brooks Atkinson in the *New York Times* seemed a little more detached: 'Mr Gielgud's Hamlet lacks a solid body of overpowering emotion, the command, power, and storm of Elizabethan tragedy. For intellectual beauty it ranks with the best, but there is a coarser ferocity to Shakespeare's tragedy that is wanting in Mr Gielgud's art.'

Those of us too young to have seen this particular Prince of Denmark then, or in his last portrayal in 1944, share the actor's regret that he turned down Alexander Korda's offer to capture it on film; though many will have made a point of catching the 1948 radio performance, which was re-broadcast by the BBC to mark Sir John's 85th birthday in 1989.

But I have skipped the year between the two Hamlets on

opposite sides of the Atlantic. In 1935 we come to his famous *Romeo and Juliet*, which he directed and in which he and Laurence Olivier alternated as Mercutio and Romeo. Motley's fluid setting allowed each scene to flow into the next, so that the play did not exceed the 'two hours' traffic of our stage' promised by the Chorus in the Prologue. Opinion is divided on the play, Hazlitt's insistence that 'Romeo is Hamlet in love' directly contradicted by Granville-Barker's 'Romeo is not a younger Hamlet in love.' Opinions were now also divided on the relative merits of the two Romeos and two Mercutios. For some Olivier was the more passionate Romeo and Gielgud the more brilliant Mercutio; on his first visit, Agate could not resist a pun: 'Mr Olivier's Romeo showed himself very much in love but rather butchered the poetry, whereas Mr Gielgud carves the verse so exquisitely that you would say the shop he kept was a *bonne-boucherie*.'

Fuller notices are reproduced in Appendix I to help readers come to their own judgment. But it is worth quoting here the conclusion of *The Times'* review after Gielgud had yielded Mercutio and launched into Romeo:

> The special interest of Mr Gielgud's work is that he has deliberately avoided what would have been, for him, the easy way to succeed in it. He is, thank heaven, a naturally romantic actor; he might, if he had pleased, have exaggerated Mr Gielgud and, by this simple process, have set the gallery in an easy blaze. But he is, happily, an artist, and has chosen a more difficult way, proving Romeo in the poetry of character rather than proclaiming him in the extravagance of personal affectations. Romeo's thought and nature appear at once, even in the early, difficult couplets, and are continually elucidated afresh, so that, when enchantment comes, reason and knowledge support it. There has seldom been better proof that, in acting, austerity of method and warmth of effect

> may run together. When the enchantment is established it is complete, and one remembers – how rarely does that remembrance spring from the stage! – that this supreme tragedy and the Sonnets were written by the same man.

When the Broadway run of *Hamlet* ended in 1937 Gielgud returned home and was soon caught up in planning his first season of classical plays as an actor-manager. He assembled a brilliant company, brought in Tyrone Guthrie and Michel St-Denis to direct the two middle plays (*The School for Scandal*, and *The Three Sisters*), appeared in all four plays at the Queen's Theatre, and also directed the two Shakespeare plays that opened and closed the season. Each play was rehearsed for eight weeks – an unheard-of luxury at that time – and ran for ten. This approach produced a level of ensemble playing that entranced audiences and critics, who admired the teamwork as much as the individual performances.

Ivor Brown praised the experiment and acquitted so scrupulous an artist of any charge of egotism: 'Mr John Gielgud is not only a fine actor himself, but a source of fine acting in others whom he can train to discover some gold of character in what is usually only the conventional base metal of the Bankside rhetoric. Mr Gielgud permits none to be a bore, emptily rattling his iambics with his armour. He elicits meaning where others leave secondary parts to mouth.'

W.A. Darlington also singled out his belief in the well-found cast rather than the star actor (though a glance at the cast-lists in Appendix V reveals Gielgud's gift for discovering actors who later became stars in their own right). In the opening production of *Richard II* Darlington almost felt inclined to take his acting for granted and devote his praise to his work as producer: 'With how masterly a touch, for example, does he let us know before a word has been spoken in the play that we are in the presence of a Court at odds with itself. Turbulence, mistrust and revolt hang heavy in the air. When the action begins we are already prepared for sinister and violent events. Some of the credit for this must go to Motley's settings, which generate atmosphere like a thundercloud.'

It was eight years since Gielgud had first attracted attention at the Old Vic in this part, and he now laid greater stress on the artist without losing any of the kingliness. Critics who had seen both interpretations thought that the new one had gained in depth, subtlety, insight and power. The last act was seen as the peak of his achievement to date: 'probably the best piece of Shakespearean acting on the English stage today.' *The Times* saw his whole performance as a movement towards that climax, and its review is reproduced in full in Appendix I.

The glamour of Richard II was in dramatic contrast to the way in which Gielgud approached Shylock. By eschewing grand histrionics he created a human and credible figure for Stephen Williams of the *Evening Standard*; but Lionel Hale in the *News Chronicle* was very disappointed: 'His Shylock reaches for no height, and touches none. Shylock is a great actor's part, a thing to colour and design. Mr Gielgud photographs it.'

Agate stooped to sarcasm:

> One could find many things to say in favour of this performance. One could praise its measure, restraint, intellectuality, if one thought that these qualities ought to be in Shylock. But suppose one holds that what the part calls for is hatred and demonic fury? Suppose one sees Shylock as storm-centre, malignant and terrible, ready to shatter the inconsiderable world about him? What, then, holding this view, is one to say of a Shylock who is merely a wet blanket at a party?

Sir John explains in this book why he feels his conception did not appeal to the audience then. But that did not prevent the

1937–8 Queen's season returning a handsome profit and engraving itself in theatrical history.

As the clouds of war gathered Gielgud turned again to Hamlet in two historic locations. The first was The Lyceum, the last production to tread the boards of Irving's famous theatre before it was turned into a dance-hall; the second was Elsinore itself, within the walls of Kronborg castle. When war broke out he toured with a recital, *Shakespeare in Peace and War*, then courageously re-opened the Old Vic with *King Lear*.

This was the production which was, in effect, produced by Harley Granville-Barker (though he refused to take that credit away from Lewis Casson in the programme). He inspired the actors with his insight into the play, and above all into the motivation of the title-role, in only ten days of rehearsals. Those of his notes to the actors that survive are reproduced in Appendix III, revealing the extraordinarily detailed nuances of his line-readings. *The Times*' review captures its impact on the audience.

Granville-Barker had shown Gielgud how to play the King not as an oak-tree riven by the thunderbolts of fate, but as an ash. James Agate, however, could not be reconciled to this conception of the rôle.

> I hope it is not mean to say that the present Lear is an ash-tree storm-tossed with infinite grace, whereas the sturdier oak has no need of graces. Mr Gielgud composes a noble head for the part, though a little less grand than Blake would have drawn. I do not feel that this Lear's rages go beyond extreme petulance – they do not frighten me! – and I am not made apprehensive by his 'I would not be mad!' because the actor does not make me feel that he is in danger of madness. . . . You would be wrong to say – this is not King Lear! You would be right to say that this is the King every inch but one.

The *Observer* worried about the effects in the storm-scene, but admired the central performance:

> Mr Gielgud's King is finely splenetive at the start, a bushy-browed martinet, acid with the sourness of age and only coming, by calamity, towards that ripeness of which the mental ruin was at last to rob him. A fiery beginning, then, with superb pathos in the first apprehensions of insanity. 'Not mad, sweet heaven!' Mr Gielgud, as he rings the bell with his rages, wrings the heart with his sense of oncoming infirmity in body and brain.

Alan Dent in the *Manchester Guardian* also found himself deeply moved by the performance: 'The first act is nothing short of superb and in the last three there is a depth of pathos which we have never had much reason to suspect before. This acting gives us much of the terror of the play, and still more the pity of it.'

When he wondered if such a tragedy of despair was quite the right choice at a time when the country faced the prospect of standing alone against the might of Hitler, Gielgud was quickly reassured by individual observers of the performance that they had found the experience cathartic, being uplifted rather than dragged down into gloom.

He followed *Lear* with a short run of *The Tempest* at the Old Vic, directed by George Devine and Marius Goring. Ivor Brown welcomed his fresh interpretation: 'Mr Gielgud's Prospero, very far from the usual mixture of Father Christmas, a Colonial Bishop, and the President of the Magician's Union, is a clear arresting picture of a virile Renaissance notable (no dotard) who has "a daily beauty in his life" as well as magic powers.'

After a break with several modern plays, he returned to Shakespeare with a long run of *Macbeth* on tour before bringing it to London in July 1942 at the Piccadilly. Michael Ayrton's designs, which set the play in the age of illuminated missals, were generally admired, and the production brought the stage 'thrillingly alive'. Gielgud's own performance was described as 'incomparable', and 'truly exciting'.

By now the *Observer* was beginning to find it difficult to discover fresh encomiums for the actor: 'That he soliloquised like a master, apostrophised superbly, and lighted the way to dusty death with the percipience of a poet go without saying.'

Agate praised his appearance, 'gaunt and sombre like an El Greco', his verse-speaking, and the magnificent virtuosity of his playing of the banquet scene, where he went all out:

> Contrary to most Macbeths, with whom going all out means petering out the rest of the way, Mr Gielgud went on to finer achievement in the immensely difficult Apparition Scene, and overtopped this by holding together those final fragments in which, if anybody is in danger of going to pieces, it is Shakespeare. All of which shows the command by this actor of immense reserves of nervous force, to which one must add imaginative control.

Alan Dent believed he had never played with more finesse, subtlety, poetry, fire, clearness and authority, and *The Times* praised his power to express fine shades of differing emotions; but the *New Statesman and Nation* thought he had rather gone over the top:

> Mr Gielgud, whose voice is a magnificent organ, treats it like a Wurlitzer, pulling out different stops in every other word. These ornamentations vulgarise the harmony just as the pauses and syncopations wreck the melody. There is hardly a line in which the rise and fall of the verse are preserved, and never a passage in which an attempt is not made to improve upon Shakespeare's incomparably varied versifications.

> Mr Gielgud can, we know, speak blank verse very finely; but often in this production one seemed to be listening to a cruel skit in a revue upon his mannerisms.

After this long and exhausting tour, with its attendant bad luck that makes one realise why actors have been superstitious about 'the Scottish Play', Gielgud turned for lighter relief to Wilde, Shaw and Congreve; but he was then prevailed upon to repeat the 1937 Queen's Theatre experience, this time with a season of five plays at the Haymarket. Again he appeared in every play, opening in *Love for Love,* followed by Somerset Maugham's *The Circle,* two Shakespeares – *Hamlet* and *A Midsummer Night's Dream* – and ending with *The Duchess of Malfi.*

What the Prince of Denmark may have lost in youthful appeal seems to have been more than made up by the power and depth of his maturity. In his review James Agate traced the development of the Gielgud Hamlets from the first to the latest and thought it now 'the best Hamlet of our time' (see Appendix I). The *Observer* praised its lucidity, and thought that the producer George Rylands had made even the Scandinavian politics intelligible and exciting: 'Mr Gielgud's Hamlet has matured without becoming over-ripe. It has everything of the Prince, from an antic disposition to a good prose style. (It is sometimes overlooked that Hamlet's prose was as good as his poetry.) It has poise and it has nerves, it has fantasy and frenzy.'

The Times saw that the actor had brought a completely fresh approach to the part he knew so well, and in which he had previously succeeded in four different productions:

> Now Mr Gielgud appears to have discovered a Hamlet whose busy, curious, hedonistic temperament is unsuited either to the demands of his mission or to any affairs which do not happen to commend themselves to an artist in life. His performance has taken on a new artificiality, and occasionally

> Hamlet suggests the actor who likes acting with passionate intensity but can scarcely bear to play the part for which he has been cast.

The Dream which followed was nowhere near so successful, and did not really satisfy either the actors or the public. There was criticism of the loss of Mendelssohn's music, and in the *Evening News* Beverley Baxter attacked the addition of Frederick Ashton's duet for Oberon and Titania: 'The formulism of fairy-land was further emphasised when Mr Gielgud and Miss Ashcroft did a ballroom dance. One, two, three, twirl, one, two, three, twirl. Just as I hoped they were going to do a rumba, it degenerated into a minuet, and then with a smile and a kingly gesture Mr Gielgud dismissed the lady.'

At the end of the season *Hamlet* departed on an ENSA tour of the Far East, where the company was thrilled by the excited response of the troops, many of whom had never seen the play and were held throughout in a high state of suspense.

A gap of four years then intervened before, in 1950, Gielgud and Shakespeare were reunited on stage, this time at Stratford-on-Avon. At Anthony Quayle's invitation he went to lead the company, in a distinct echo of Lilian Baylis's invitation to go to the Old Vic twenty years before. He opened in Peter Brook's production of *Measure for Measure,* the first of several memorable collaborations. *The Times* thought him intellectually unsparing as the Angelo whose 'blood is very snow-broth':

> ... that hollow pillar, the hypocrite self-betrayed. He does not fret the part into a pathological study: but his mind is clear before us. There can be nothing but pity at the last when the man, no longer speaking like an icy flame, bows before the Duke with 'Immediate sentence then, and sequent death, is all the grace I beg'. Peter Brook, whose production throughout is both swift and legitimately inventive, has

> clarified the complexities of the last act. Few will forget its charged and daring pause before Isabella pleads for the life of Angelo.

In the second production he at last played Cassius, the part he had long coveted in *Julius Caesar*, and surprised himself and the company by the torrent of his passion on the opening night. J.C. Trewin welcomed the play's return, after a period of neglect, as like a strong draught of wine:

> At the première I knew that all was safe with the evening as soon as John Gielgud's Cassius began to urge Brutus to the edge. This scene proved to be one of the noblest feats of declamation in my experience. Though I recognised Gielgud's quality as a Shakespearean, I did not expect this leaping blaze of speech. He has been the principal violin of our stage. Here now, as Cassius, he moves one like the Coronation trumpets in the Abbey.

(A prophetic metaphor – his knighthood was announced three years later in the Coronation Honours List.)

Alan Dent put his possession of the part more succinctly: 'Mr Gielgud is thoroughly inside the character. Three or four times he looks not so much *at* as *into* the audience, and we observe that his eyes have the curious sightless blaze of a man obsessed with an ideal.' Two years later he repeated this electrifying performance in the Hollywood film directed by Joseph Mankiewicz.

Next, Gielgud took over the part of Benedick from Anthony Quayle in his own production of *Much Ado About Nothing*, revived from the previous year. It was to be revived again and again over the rest of the decade, with three different Beatrices – Peggy Ashcroft, Diana Wynyard, and Margaret Leighton – and always seeming to preserve a perennial freshness. W.A.

Darlington recognised the difficulties in getting the balance right between the two salty-tongued lovers and the rest of the plot, which 'nobody has ever got more exactly right, I feel sure, than Mr Gielgud.' He thought Benedick one of his best comic creations. The *Sketch* had never seen such elegance and gaiety; even in the silence of Benedick in the arbour 'Gielgud listens as wittily as he speaks'. Harold Hobson in the *Sunday Times* was delighted that 'now we are having his glad, confident youth all over again'. And Anthony Cookman in the *Tatler* disputed one of Agate's earlier criticisms: 'He is, contrary to opinion once general, such a very good comic actor. He is as quick to apprehend a fine shade of humour as to apprehend a fine shade of tragedy, and his usual method of expressing it is to deepen the gravity which sits naturally on his stage appearance. The gravity with which his Benedick reasons himself into a resolution to fall in love with Beatrice is exquisitely comic.'

Gielgud ended the 1950 Stratford season with a return to *Lear*, maintaining his loyalty to the Granville-Barker conception of ten years earlier, and co-directing it with Anthony Quayle. Ivor Brown's review was headed 'Every Inch a King', and commended the way in which he gave no embroidery of character-acting as Olivier's Lear had done. He thought it a tremendous as well as a poignant Lear: 'As a physical and vocal feat it was impressive; as proof that Gielgud can enlarge his style with the years it is the best of news. That he would triumph in the final pathos one could assume; the test of a Lear is the start, and in this, with his ripe, kingly authority, he was no less excellent.'

The following year he approached another unfamiliar play, *The Winter's Tale*, under the guidance of Peter Brook's direction and, as the *Observer* put it, 'turning the No. 2 Shakespearean parts into No. 1 achievements'. The *Spectator*, too, overcame its reservations about the structural defects of the play because Peter Brook had brought out the strength in it: 'Most of this stems from Mr Gielgud's very fine performance as Leontes, whose jealousy is so unquestionably real and terrible that we are not worried by the fact that its causes are flimsy and its consequences far-fetched.'

The *Illustrated London News* recognised the difficulties for the actor playing Leontes, who launches into a gale of jealous rage almost as soon as he appears on the stage: 'John Gielgud establishes Leontes immediately; no other actor in my recollection has turned this gnarled verse to music, and Gielgud manages to touch us deeply as the tyrant in repentance. At the close there is grave beauty in reconciliation.'

T.C. Worsley felt the actor was discovering in himself new depths of feeling and ranges of voice, and Richard Findlater shared that perception: 'It is a virtuoso performance, theatrically expert in conception and execution and the verse is spoken with subtle lucidity and delicate balance. But this is something more than a technical feat: it has the profundity of common experience, lit by the incandescent fire of maturing genius.'

It was this performance that prompted Kenneth Tynan to capture the spirit of Gielgud's ability to hold an audience in thrall: 'His voice thrills like an arrow, shot skywards: it rarely touches the gruff phrases of earth. Now, as we listen, it flies higher still, until it hits a resonant, alto headnote. This is its climax.'

Its audience appeal was such that it set a Shakespearean record for the longest run of the play, beating the previous best of 166 performances set by Forbes-Robertson at the Lyceum in 1887.

The Gielgud sure touch deserted him in the 'Japanese Lear' designed by Isamu Noguchi in 1955. The critics echoed the King's line to Edgar: 'I do not like the fashion of your garments: you will say they are Persian; but let them be changed.' The *Daily Sketch* proclaimed that Lear looked like a Gruyère cheese;

the *Illustrated London News* thought the tragedy was ruined and Gielgud's Lear hampered at every move:

> Sir John appears before us nearly smothered in a vast hanging fringe of white beard, wearing upon his head a knobbly crown of uncompromising ugliness, and carrying what looks like an eccentric hearth-brush. He holds court in a palace (Scene: Britain) that has more to do with Euclid than Shakespeare. And he is most oddly attended by courtiers who wear queer coif-and-portcullis outfits, and who are obviously from some tall story of science fiction. It is a dangerous beginning, and the night soon falls about us in shreds. The costumes, with their Japanese suggestions, thrust our minds as far from *Lear* as possible. . . . In short, all elaborate and distracting where it should have been simple and basic. The pity of it is that Gielgud's Lear has suffered in the same way.

After this it was a relief to many that Peter Brook wrought his magic again with *The Tempest* in 1957 at Stratford and then at Drury Lane. Philip Hope-Wallace in the *Guardian* asserted: 'When it comes to the greatest of Shakespearean speeches, Sir John Gielgud has no peer. . . . Two other Gielgud Prosperos are recalled. This third reading is wonderfully clear of insipidity of boredom. Here is no bearded wizard but an exile, the hurt, watchful outcast, first cousin of Timon of Athens but heading towards serenity and release.'

Kenneth Tynan took the opportunity to hone the sharpness of one of his most famous double-edged compliments, when he commended this spare, ascetic Prospero:

> Instead of a venerable Mosaic figure, we have an austere and bookish hermit, who wears a brief, mud-coloured toga and whose life is wholly of mind. At first Sir John seemed embarrassed by his semi-nudity ('The costumes,' one felt him

> signalling, 'are arriving tomorrow'), but he went on to give one of his best abstract performances. Bodily inexpressive and manually gauche, he is perhaps the finest actor, from the neck up, in the world today. His face is all rigour and pain, his voice all cello and woodwind: the rest of him is totem pole. But he speaks the great passages perfectly, and always looks full of thinking. The part demands no more.

W.A. Darlington, less reserved in his view of both play and player, hailed an outstanding achievement by the actor in creating such a vital figure of mysterious power: 'Sir John has given me the first Prospero that I have ever seen who, I feel, might have satisfied Shakespeare.' J.C. Trewin's judgment is reproduced in full in Appendix I.

The following year saw the Old Vic complete its five year cycle of all Shakespeare's plays of the First Folio with a star-studded production by Michael Benthall of *Henry VIII*, in which the royal pair were played by Harry Andrews and Edith Evans; Gielgud was Wolsey, 'the very pinnacle of proud disdain', as Darlington put it. Not natural casting for the low-born 'butcher's boy', he used other attributes to flesh out the character, as *The Times* perceived:

> The showpiece of the evening is Sir John's masterly handling of the transformation that takes place in the character of Wolsey on his downfall. The actor does not trouble to search at the height of the Cardinal's ostentatious pride for hints that might prepare us for a change of heart. He draws the scheming prelate in harsh, sharp lines as a ruthlessly acquisitive, hateful, inordinately ambitious figure animated with forceful malevolence; and then, suddenly, with little or no preparation and with overwhelming pathos, reveals the man's other self which has been waiting to discover 'the blessedness of being little'.

In 1959 Gielgud took *Much Ado* to North America on its final tour, and at the end of its run in New York spoke for the first time of giving up acting entirely and devoting himself to directing. Happily for his audiences he did not carry out that threat. In this period of uncertainty, when it seemed difficult for him to find the right play, he toured the world with his *Ages of Man* Shakespeare recital, which continually drew audiences from 1957 to 1967. Milton Shulman found King Lear in a bow-tie distracting, but Richard Findlater saw this one-man show as a testament to the power and beauty of the word, and Harold Hobson applauded his appearance on one summit of Shakespeare's verse after another, without ever descending to the intervening valleys. T.C. Worsley paid tribute to the truthfulness of the performance: 'What is so admirable about Sir John is that he places his gifts – of voice, intelligence, of understanding, of sympathy – completely at the service of the work he is interpreting.'

In the Sixties he made only two other forays into Shakespeare, with neither of which was he particularly happy. The first was his 1961 Othello at Stratford, directed by Zeffirelli, who hampered his cast with difficult costumes and enormous sets, parts of which wobbled disconcertingly on the first night. The critics were quick to say this Moor was inappropriately cast, from Penelope Gilliatt in *Queen* ('Far from suggesting that he could eat Desdemona raw for breakfast, he makes one feel he would really like her served on a tray in the library') to Kenneth Tynan in the *Observer* ('Gielgud himself is quite simply over-parted. In his hands Othello dwindles into a coffee-stained Leontes; instead of a wounded bull, dangerous despite its injuries, we have a heraldic eagle with its wings harmlessly clipped').

But *The Times* saluted his courage in a leader column, saying 'a case can be argued for great actors unwilling to play safe', arguing that our distrust of rhetoric makes it difficult for us to accept Othello's view of himself, though not the psychological depths of this fallen hero: 'When such mastery is combined in one actor with exceptional command of the tones, rhythms, and tempo of blank verse, it becomes almost a duty to measure himself against Othello.'

In 1964 he returned to *Hamlet* to direct Richard Burton in the modern-dress 'rehearsal-clothes' production on Broadway. It had a mixed critical reception, but it was such a sell-out with audiences that it beat Sir John's own record run set in 1937.

Since the 1961 *Othello*, Gielgud has appeared in only two stage performances in Shakespeare, both for the National Theatre. The first was at the Old Vic in Peter Hall's production of *The Tempest* in 1974 (it was also the first by the new director since he had succeeded Laurence Olivier). In one particularly striking visual effect at the end, Prospero removed his cap to speak the Epilogue, startling the audience with his sudden resemblance to Shakespeare's portrait, as Irving Wardle describes in his long and perceptive review (see Appendix I).

By the time Gielgud played the title-role in *Julius Caesar* in 1977 the National Theatre had moved into its new building, and he was unhappy with the acoustic of the large Olivier auditorium. John Schlesinger's production was savaged by several critics, and Michael Billington in the *Guardian* attacked the conspiracy as 'a gratuitous attempt to kill off the best verse-speaker on the English stage'. B.A. Young said 'John Gielgud's Caesar bestrides the production like a Colossus, with impecc-ably spoken verse and subtle characterisation.' J.C. Trewin felt that this Caesar did indeed govern Rome, and that the audience was able to sense the man's greatness as well as the qualities that doomed him. Bernard Levin commented that 'the proud full sail of the verse' was in short supply except in Gielgud's mouth:

> ... all the music of that unique *vibrato* is deployed in a performance of the utmost nobility, a passage like
>
> And tell them that I will not come today:
> Cannot is false, and that I dare not, falser
>
> would send a thrill through anyone with enough imagination to wonder what it would have been like to be in the conqueror's presence, and Gielgud's majesty is sustained right through to his dreamlike appearance as the ghost, which leaves his 'Ay, at Philippi' hovering in the air like some infinitely shimmering echo.
>
> 'Here was a Caesar! When comes such another?'

His Shakespearean film performances have been regrettably few. Apart from Cassius in the 1953 Hollywood *Caesar* we have his Prologue in Renato Castellani's *Romeo and Juliet* (1954), his Clarence in the Olivier *Richard III* (1955), his King Henry IV in Orson Welles' *Chimes at Midnight* (1966), and Julius Caesar in 1970 for Stuart Burge.

For television he has again played the Prologue to *Romeo and Juliet* twice, (1967 and 1978) and John of Gaunt in *Richard II* (1978). For BBC Radio he has broadcast *The Tempest* five times, *Hamlet* four times, *King Lear* three times, and *Othello, Richard II, Henry V* and *The Winter's Tale* once each; in addition he has made commercial recordings of *Hamlet, Henry V, Julius Caesar, Measure For Measure, Much Ado About Nothing, Othello, Richard II, Richard III*, and *The Winter's Tale*.

His most recent Shakespeare performance was in many ways the most demanding, but having waited so long to bring *The Tempest* to the screen it may well be that *Prospero's Books* will prove to be the most rewarding for the actor and the audience. His subjective reactions to his own performances are not always the same as those who observe them, and I was frequently surprised by his observations on the plays, the characters, and his own interpretations, but I never ceased to find them illuminating, and I hope and believe the reader will be as stimulated and enlightened as I was.

CHAPTER ONE

Directing • The Old Vic • *Hamlet*

When I first became ambitious to play some of the great Shakespearean parts, I tried to profit by reading all I could about them. I have read voraciously all my life, though I have always been apt to gallop far too quickly through the enormous quantity of material that I ought to have taken time to digest fully. But I think I did manage to pick up a certain amount of information. My shelves are crammed with theatre books of every kind – Brandes and Bradley, Caroline Spurgeon, and especially the Granville-Barker prefaces, which I have always found so infinitely useful and constructive. I still delight in reading many of the critics who have written so finely on Shakespeare – Shaw and Max Beerbohm, Hazlitt, George Lewes, and, in my own time, Kenneth Tynan, J.C. Trewin, Ivor Brown, James Agate, and John Masefield, with whom I was once lucky enough to discuss *Macbeth* (and whose brief summary of the plots of each play I persuaded Harcourt Williams to use in the programmes at the Old Vic) – besides countless biographies of Irving and Ellen Terry, Kean, Garrick, Macready, and many others. I do not recall when I began to understand the functions of a director, but it must have been in the early Twenties, when I first acted in Chekhov under Theodore Komisarjevsky. And when he directed *King Lear* for the Oxford undergraduates I was greatly impressed by his work in Shakespeare. I was less satisfied with his *Macbeth* later at

Stratford, though there were strikingly effective moments in it. But I never saw his other controversial productions there – *The Merchant of Venice, The Comedy of Errors* (and, I think, *The Merry Wives of Windsor*) – nor his later London production of *Antony and Cleopatra*, which was a miscast and, apparently, disastrous venture. I wonder if my admiration for his encouragement and perception would have been equally inspiring if I had worked for him in Shakespeare.

After the death of Herbert Beerbohm Tree, whose productions at His Majesty's I never saw, there were not many managements in London daring to compete with his legend. J.B. Fagan, who directed a number of Shakespeare plays in his 1920 seasons at the Royal Court, was not helped by his wife, who appeared in all the plays; but he gave opportunities to one or two fine actors – Maurice Moscovitch as Shylock, for instance, and Godfrey Tearle in his first Othello. But Fagan was fairly conventional in the directing of his productions, with too many scene changes and rather timid attempts to break away from the traditions of Benson and Beerbohm Tree.

I do not think the John Barrymore *Hamlet* in 1925 was credited to any official director. He had brought over the production from New York with its beautiful permanent setting by Robert Edmond Jones (marred only by too many steps and several front-scenes played before flimsy curtains) – and no doubt Barrymore himself had put the rather uneven English company through their paces when he arrived, as the old actor managers always did. I was told that Sir Johnston Forbes-Robertson – the most celebrated Hamlet after Henry Irving – came to one of the rehearsals, presumably to tender his advice to Barrymore.

John Barrymore was 45 when he played Hamlet in London. The old actor-managers had always graduated to the part when they were no longer young. Forbes-Robertson was quite middle-aged when he first appeared in it. Irving played it when he was fairly young, but never revived it afterwards. At the age of 25 my own youth was a great advantage. It seemed to make the early scenes more poignant, particularly Hamlet's grief for his father.

As a boy I was lucky enough to see the last of Granville-Barker's Savoy productions, *A Midsummer Night's Dream*, and I loved every moment of it, without having the slightest idea of the way in which it would revolutionise my view of the way Shakespeare could really come alive as it did for me at the Old Vic in 1929. Harcourt Williams, our director there, was a wonderfully easy man to work for, and he gave me so many great opportunities that I feel rather ungenerous in saying that, though he was a dedicated artist with extremely good taste, enchanting modesty, and boundless enthusiasm, he was not sensationally inspired as a director. Still, with the appalling restrictions he had to face when he came to the Vic, he managed to accomplish wonders of ingenuity in every kind of emergency and was a tower of encouragement to me, and it was entirely due to his influence that, at the end of my Vic seasons, I became determined to try and direct a Shakespeare play myself.

In the early Twenties, when I was still at RADA, I had seen a number of simple but effective Shakespeare productions at the Vic, under Robert Atkins (a boozy old survivor of the days of Forbes-Robertson and Beerbohm Tree), who managed a shabby, ill-paid company with extraordinary skill and enterprise. He succeeded in mounting *Peer Gynt* (in which I was a super), a remarkably ambitious achievement (with Russell Thorndike as Peer) and I spoke my very first line on the professional stage in his production of *Henry V*, as well as walking on (unpaid of course) in *King Lear** and a play about Wat Tyler.

* I remember trying to keep a straight face as I was holding my spear in the first act of *King Lear*, when that charming actor Austin Trevor, who was playing Edmund, whispered to me: 'Look at that dear old man in the front row, holding his copy of the play and trying to follow the cuts.'

As an 18-year-old boy I was naturally terrified of both Atkins himself and his ill-paid and somewhat provincial company, but I could already sense the responsive enthusiasm of the Old Vic audiences, and the cosy atmosphere of the shabby old theatre which managed to prosper under the somewhat domineering perseverance of Lilian Baylis.

As a student I had seen *Richard II* with Ernest Milton at the Old Vic and fallen in love with the part long before I had the chance of playing it myself. But it was not until I learnt the lines and rehearsed them in three short weeks that I had any idea what the character was really like. For Benedick, on the other hand, I have never been rightly cast, and I did not expect to have any success with it. I knew I would not be able to be very convincing as the bluff soldier, and felt I made a somewhat daring experiment in taking it on. I enjoyed playing Hotspur, too, although I doubted if I had the guns for it, and I even attempted Antony in *Antony and Cleopatra,* for which of course I was utterly unsuited. But I padded my doublet and wore a false beard and shouted and boomed and seemed to get some sort of result.

I remember thinking I could not learn the lines because there were whole speeches that I did not understand, and there was no time to discuss them or to go and look them up in the Variorum (the speech for instance 'Like boys unto a muss, Kings would start forth and cry, Your will?'). But I tried to learn about punctuation and breathing. It seemed to me that if you were not quite sure of a very difficult speech in Shakespeare, and you studied the punctuation and got it right, the sense would in some way emerge. Much later, in both *The Winter's Tale* and *Measure For Measure,* I was alarmed to find that so much of the verse was very obscure; but I tried to trust to the sweep of every speech, and to mark the commas and full stops and semi-colons, and if I observed these correctly, as a bad swimmer begins to trust the water, the text seemed to hold me up.

One of the things I found from playing my two seasons at the Old Vic was that, having so little time (three weeks' rehearsal and then only about thirteen performances of each play), one simply had to trust the verse. There was no time to examine the text in detail or discuss motivation – something that American actors love so much (and a great many English directors love, too). But I have never believed that long sessions of talk beforehand from an intellectual point of view are ever very constructive. The important thing is to bring the play over the footlights to the audience. Certainly that was what the Old Vic used to cater for in its cheap old days, drawing a very working-class audience and a few young intellectuals and students, who seemed happy to accept the plays just as they were given them. We didn't try to do anything very subtle or highbrow because there was never time, and we flew at our work in a very straightforward way, trusting to our own enthusiasm and the guidance of Harcourt Williams, who not only gave us a great deal of freedom but was also a model of energy, persuasiveness and tact.

The tendency with Shakespeare before my day had been to give the actor-manager the limelight and the centre of the stage, with all the small parts just standing about giving cues. The small parts in Shakespeare are very often quite roughly indicated, but if they are wonderfully acted, (Olivier as Shallow, George Devine as Peter in *Romeo and Juliet*, or Alec Guinness as Osric), you suddenly find they can come to life in a surprisingly effective way. It is never beneath an actor's dignity to play the smaller parts in Shakespeare.

I have directed at least fifty plays in my long career, eight of them by Shakespeare, and came to enjoy doing so quite as much as acting in them, though I also appeared in many of the productions myself. I have never been given much critical credit for my work as a director. But I know I was good at casting, and enormously happy working with both actors and designers. I think I managed to create a good atmosphere at rehearsals, which is so important, and did not pontificate or bully the players, though they were often inclined to be justly put out when I was too hasty and changeable and fond of contradicting myself at their expense.

Komisarjevsky and Michel St-Denis were both tremendous influences for me; and at a critical time, much later in my career, I was extraordinarily lucky to be directed by Peter Brook, Lindsay Anderson and Peter Hall. All these men were fine teachers as well as splendid directors and sympathetic colleagues, and I shall always be grateful for their help. Being rehearsed in *Lear* by the great Granville-Barker, (though, alas, only for a few days) was an unforgettable experience, but in my very early days Nigel Playfair was the only director who gave me real help, and I was more influenced by some of the actors whom I was lucky enough to work with, such as Noël Coward, Lilian Braithwaite and Leslie Faber, who took the trouble to criticise my acting with perceptive kindliness. Fortunately I also had a number of private friends who refused to flatter me even when I was beginning to be successful; and though of course I made some enemies and was to experience quite a lot of mistakes and failures, I was very lucky in my contracted seasons, first under Bronson Albery and then with Hugh Beaumont, in which I was given a very free hand in casting and direction as well as being consulted over the choice of plays and the subsequent productions of them.

In his book *Four Years at The Old Vic* Harcourt Williams wrote that when I first played Lear my 'odd twist to the neck, as if the head were too heavy for it, gave at once a sense of mental danger.' When you are acting well, people imagine all sorts of things that you never even thought of. In *Hamlet*, particularly, many people credited me with touches that I was not even aware of myself. I could hardly read Rosamond Gilder's detailed book about my performance. It seemed terribly boring to read in cold blood at what line I turned my head or dropped my dagger or sat in a chair. Though of course while you are playing you do take careful notice of what you are doing, there are so many thoughts running through your head all the time you are acting that you hardly know which of them are the most important. You have to be so aware of what you are doing that when you do something good you remember it, and when you do something bad you remember that, too, and try to cut it out at the next performance.

It is always very difficult to know who to listen to, whose advice to take – even that of the director who, having to see the performance so often, may find it hard to judge you dispassionately after a time. After a production has been running for some time, a director may come back to see a performance (though few directors come back often enough, in my opinion); but by then it is extremely hard (both for him and for you) to readjust. Granville-Barker used to say that a good production should be kept in a repertoire for many years. I have always thought that was an impossible idea unless the cast was changed from time to time and the director was prepared to supervise continually and rehearse things carefully again. When a play is put aside for several performances in repertory, the actors take it up rather nervously five or six nights later, only to find quite often that the whole thing has got out of key and needs to be rehearsed again more thoroughly. This of course needs great discipline and hard work. In *Hamlet* I used to think 'Well, I'm playing this part again, I must do it better this time. Shall I try to remember what was good that I did before? No, better not think of that, but try to find something new. But how to do that now that I'm so much older than when I first conceived the part and had the youthful attributes that went with it?' I would be assailed by all sorts of contradictory confusions in my mind, while trying to marshall the physical energy to go through the exhausting action and keeping the correct positions, stance, audibility, and pace that I had worked out at rehearsal. On the nights when the play possessed me, I occasionally felt I could forget all these complicated feelings; but of course this very rarely happened.

When I devised the solo recital *Ages of Man*, I discovered that, in doing speeches out of their proper context, I had to remember that in every speech there was a rise, a climax and a fall, having in my mind where I was going to and where I was coming from, and then I could put any amount of variations in between (as musicians often do in playing Chopin, for instance) while keeping the essential architecture of each speech intact.

Truth is what we all strive for in acting. Yet acting can never be truth, it has to seem to be truthful, but carefully observed, selected, and then conveyed to the audience in movement, costume, voice, and action.

I played in five or six productions of *Hamlet* over fifteen years – an extraordinary piece of luck for any actor. But many people said that my original performance in 1930 was the best, because I had no idea I was going to be good. When you get some sort of reputation behind you it is much harder to live up to it, and far more dangerous. Also, you are afraid of becoming a bit too pleased with yourself. The only thing that gives you satisfaction is to work with new actors around you and a new director who will not allow you to do many of the things you did before.

Granville-Barker believed that there is something in the part of Claudius to be found more highly developed in Macbeth. (And I think there is something of the same kind in Brutus, too, which Shakespeare was to develop later in both Hamlet and Macbeth.) Claudius is a wonderful part (Alfred Lunt said he would always have liked to play it), and I rather fancied it myself when I got older, though the part is usually heavily cut because the play is so long.

When I played *Hamlet* on Broadway in 1936, I had reservations about the casting of Ophelia. I had seen Lillian Gish when I was a boy – on a poster in the Tube in London, under the caption 'Two little strangers of whom the world will soon be talking'. The picture showed two small girls wearing straw hats with ribbons in D.W. Griffith's film *Orphans of the Storm*: Lillian and Dorothy Gish. So when Guthrie McClintic (my New York director) said he was engaging her to play Ophelia with me, I asked him if she was still young enough. About three nights later (I was playing in *Richard of Bordeaux* at the time), the stage door keeper said, 'There is a lady to see you', and round the door came a pretty little hat with ribbons and Lillian Gish herself saying, 'Am I too old for Ophelia?' She turned out to be wonderfully good, especially in the mad scene, when she wore a red stocking on one arm. I acted once again with her in New York in *Crime and Punishment*, when she played the consumptive wife of Marmeladov splendidly, and we have been devoted friends ever since.

When McClintic first showed me the designs for his production I was a bit put out. I had told him I wanted to wear Tudor costume, as I had in London, with a high collar; and there it was in the drawing. But the other costumes (by Jo Mielziner) were inspired by Van Dyck. I thought them very beautiful but ventured to say 'Why not Rembrandt?' No one seemed to understand what I was driving at, and we all looked very fine in beautiful silks and velvets, but I couldn't help thinking the Rembrandt feeling of armour and fur might have been much better.

Although I had twice before directed productions of *Hamlet* in England as well as acting in them, I was sadly disappointed when I undertook to direct the play in America in 1964 for Richard Burton. He was anxious not to have to wear a period costume with tights, and told me how impressed he had been when once in London, some years before, he had seen me play Richard II in rehearsal clothes. This led me to conceive a production of *Hamlet* in modern dress on a stage with bare walls and only a few platforms and essential furniture. This turned out to be bleak and unattractive, though the production was an enormous success, and, ironically enough, played in New York for more than 100 performances, breaking my own previous record in 1937.

The opening performance was in Toronto, at the impossibly vast O'Keefe Centre with its cavernous auditorium, and during our rehearsals there Burton was married to Elizabeth Taylor. On the first night she was mobbed as she came into the stalls, and people stood on their seats to get a glimpse of her and tried to watch her reactions throughout the evening. And when we landed at Boston we were surrounded by fans, who tore at the Burtons' hair and clothes, and the plane had to be moved to another part of the airport to enable them to emerge unhurt.

I felt that my only contribution to this production that had any merit was in my treatment of the Ghost. I had a great black shadow which suddenly took shape above the stage and hovered over Hamlet throughout the scene, then slowly moved away until it disappeared. But altogether I felt that my work was untidy and ill-conceived, perhaps because I had become too familiar with the play over so many years. I should never have attempted to direct another actor in a part I knew so well myself. I made the same mistake later on when I tried to direct Ralph Richardson in *Macbeth* and Paul Scofield in *Richard II*.

In directing Burton's own performance, I said the only help I could give him was to show him how the more relaxed scenes were placed, so that, for instance, he need not tear himself to shreds in the dark in the scene with the Ghost or in various other passages between the big emotional climaxes; and this advice he seemed to find helpful. But he never seemed to want to work alone with me except on one occasion (and even then one of the cast hid in a dress basket, took notes and wrote a book about it afterwards). Of course, he had played the part before at the Old Vic.* Finally, when we were on the road before we opened in New York, I was reduced to writing long notes for him, which I would leave on his dressing table before the performance in the evening. He would read them through very quickly, discard most of my suggestions but use three or four of them during that same evening's performance without even rehearsing them. All the same he was very often instinctively right about them, and he was shrewd, generous, intelligent and co-operative. I was very fond of him. But I felt he was, finally, something of a 'Shropshire Lad' Hamlet, and I would have rather had the opportunity of working with him as either Macbeth or Coriolanus. It might have been much better for us both, I think, if we had come to *Hamlet* absolutely freshly.

I kept on saying to Burton, 'The important thing is to tell the story of the play and to make every scene a progression.' That is what Granville-Barker had once said to me about playing *Lear*: 'You must start the next scene where you left off in the last one, even if there is another scene between the two'. In *Hamlet* this is particularly important because there are so many scenes – the nunnery scene, the play scene, the closet scene, the graveyard scene – which are so well known. Every new Hamlet must link the strands of the play by an individual, original attitude, and tell the story anew for the audience. He must try to experience the progression of the play and not think which scene he needs most to worry about. He must, so to

* When I went to see his performance, we had arranged to have supper together afterwards. He took rather a long time getting changed, and I said 'I'll go on ahead. Come when you're better – I mean, when you're ready!' One of my favourite famous gaffes.

speak, not know what is coming next, and really live the part every night.

In America I found it impossibly difficult to cast the other parts for Burton's *Hamlet* because I didn't know any of the actors there. We had exhaustive auditions, but I could not make up my mind who was good and who was not, and I found that a lot of my time was wasted by actors who wanted motivation for Shakespeare's supporting parts. If I said: 'You're just meant to support Hamlet,' they were very hurt and cross. I had endless Ophelias to audition in New York, and all of them insisted on doing the mad scene. Some of them came down in outlandish costumes, and one of them gave birth to a doll from under her dress. I knew that each time there would be two parts of the scene for me to listen to, so that the audition would take eight minutes instead of five, which was just what the hopeful young ladies were counting on. And when I said I wanted them to do 'O, what a noble mind is here o'erthrown!', a far more difficult speech, I found they had not studied it at all.

How lucky I had been to have Lillian Gish in the McClintic production. I think Ophelia is one of the most difficult parts in Shakespeare. Jessica Tandy, who played it with me at the New Theatre in London in 1934, was marvellously good, though the critics thought she was too modern. It is a part that I have seldom seen very successfully played, although Fay Compton, who acted it with Barrymore in 1925 (and with me in 1939) made a great success of it, as did Peggy Ashcroft, my last Ophelia, in 1944.

The final scene in *Hamlet* is very difficult. The actors are tired, and so is the audience. Once, when I was playing the moment with Horatio just before the end and I said, 'If it be now, 'tis not to come; if it be not to come, it will be now', a man in the front row took out an enormous watch and began loudly winding it up. I could hardly go on with what I was saying.

For my own detailed notes on the playing of *Hamlet*, please refer to Appendix II.

CHAPTER TWO

Romeo and Juliet • *Richard II* • *King Lear*

In my early acting days I had got to know *Romeo and Juliet* extremely well. I first played Paris in an amateur production one Sunday night in London, while I was acting in Fagan's Repertory Theatre in Oxford. Not long after this came my engagement to play Romeo at the Regent with Gwen Ffrangcon-Davies, and then, in my first season at the Vic in 1929, we opened with the same play and I was again cast as Romeo. In the following year I was invited to direct the play at Oxford, and launched for the first time into this new field, working for the OUDS with a fine undergraduate cast headed by George Devine, and with the invaluable help, as guest-artists, of Peggy Ashcroft, playing Juliet for the first time, and Edith Evans, who had already played the Nurse at the Vic and in America, repeating her definitive performance. The three Motley girls – Margaret ('Percy') Harris, her sister Sophia and Elizabeth Montgomery – who were to be so closely associated with me in my productions for the next few years, designed the costumes (though not the scenery on this occasion).

I was then engaged by Howard Wyndham and Bronson Albery, who owned three West End theatres, with a contract for three productions, and I acted for them from 1931 to 1936 in *Musical Chairs*, *Richard of Bordeaux*, and *Hamlet* for three long and successful runs (I also directed the last two), as well as acting in *Noah* and *The Maitlands* and directing several contemporary plays (*Sheppey, Strange Orchestra,* and *The Old Ladies*).

In 1934 I had to abandon staging a new version of *A Tale of Two Cities,* which I had concocted in collaboration with Terence Rattigan. The Motleys had designed an excellent permanent set, and the cast had been chosen and approached, when I suddenly received a very forceful letter from the veteran actor-manager Sir John Martin Harvey, who had announced a farewell tour of his long acclaimed adaptation of the Dickens novel, called *The Only Way.* 'For you to usurp the part of Sidney Carton,' he wrote, 'would be like proposing to stage *The Bells* while Irving was still alive'. I sought the advice of my managers as well as that of several important dramatic critics, but they all seemed to think it would be 'taking the bread out of the old man's mouth', and I had no alternative but to abandon my project. Anxious to show in London the success I had achieved in Oxford, I suggested staging *Romeo and Juliet* again, encouraged by the fact that Peggy Ashcroft and Edith Evans were both likely to be available again to appear in it with me.

Much as I loved the part of Romeo, I knew by this time how difficult it was, and that a good Mercutio might easily eclipse me. I had once seen that happen in 1919, in a disastrous production of the play, in which the Juliet of the American actress Doris Keane and the Romeo of Basil Sydney were overshadowed by the successes of Ellen Terry as the Nurse (her last professional engagement) and Leon Quartermaine, who played Mercutio so finely. The audience had shouted for him at the end of the first night performance, but he was modest enough to slip away directly after his death scene.

I suddenly had the idea of playing Mercutio in my new production (as well as speaking the Chorus in a mask) and asking another leading man to play Romeo, with both of us changing parts after six weeks of the run.

When Robert Donat, whom I first approached with the idea,

refused, I turned to Laurence Olivier, whom I had directed some months earlier when he played Bothwell in *Queen of Scots*, which Gordon Daviot (authoress of *Richard of Bordeaux*) had written for Gwen Ffrangcon-Davies, but which had run only for a few months.

Olivier accepted my proposal enthusiastically, and we set to work. At this time his career had not fully taken off. He had made a sensational success as Stanhope in the first Sunday night performance of *Journey's End* but, as he was under contract to Basil Dean, he was not available to play the rôle again when the play was put on in the West End. That production was to prove an enormous success (with Stanhope played by Colin Clive) running in both London and America for several years.

Meanwhile, Olivier had been seen in two failures for Basil Dean, *Beau Geste* and *The Circle of Chalk*, and in two other plays, *Ringmaster* and *The Rats of Norway*. In all these productions he achieved splendid personal and critical success, though he was not the top star in any of them. He was then married to Jill Esmond and had been planning a *Romeo and Juliet* in which they would both appear. But he generously agreed to abandon his project and work with me instead. We had only a short period for rehearsal as the New Theatre would be empty and needing an attraction in a few weeks' time. The Motleys speedily and cleverly adapted the set they had already designed for the Dickens play.

To the end of his life Olivier was unable to forget the bad notices he received for his verse-speaking as Romeo, though he was too proud to mention them at the time. I knew I was more lyrically successful as Mercutio in the Queen Mab scene, but his virility and panache in the other scenes, his furious and skilful fencing and final exit to his death, were certainly more striking in the part than anything I was able to achieve, while his performance as Romeo was infinitely romantic. His beautiful pose as he stood beneath the balcony expressed the essence of the character to perfection. I was tempted to remonstrate at his insistence on wearing a false nose (he always used one whenever possible – as Puff, Shallow, and Oedipus, as well as for Richard III and Lear). I felt also that he was inclined to be too athletic in the bedroom scene with Juliet. I have always believed that too much 'physical' acting here goes against Shakespeare's intention: he so carefully devised the balcony scene as prelude, and the farewell scene as post-consummation, in order to avoid embarrassing both the boy actor who created his Juliet and the audience.

Olivier and I got on splendidly all the same, though I think he rightly felt I was inclined to show off in my verse-speaking, which was becoming too much like singing. I daresay I was somewhat smug after a few recent successes, and perhaps was inclined to patronise him from my position of authority. Only the other day I was much amused, when reading the memoirs of Lydia Lopokova (the Diaghilev ballerina who later married the economist Maynard Keynes), by a passage from a letter written to her by Frederick Ashton, famous for his sharp tongue: 'Went to the second performance of *Romeo,* Gielgud very Sarah Bernhardt [*voix d'or* I imagine he meant], Edith Evans as the Nurse quite overbalanced the production.' He did not even mention either Olivier or Peggy Ashcroft, and I hope there was not too much truth in his remarks.

Between 1920 and 1938 I became increasingly familiar with three Shakespeare plays, which I got to know almost by heart: *Romeo and Juliet, The Merchant of Venice,* and *Richard II.* I played in all of them at various times, and also directed each of them twice, with some success. At the Old Vic, of course, the budgets had always been appallingly meagre – as little as £20 was allowed to be spent on each production; scenery and costumes, properties and furniture were used over and over again, with a few changes and modifications, and had to be shared with the opera company.

I learnt a good deal from working in such conditions, but was of course delighted to be able to mount subsequent productions of my own in infinitely grander style, though I tried to curb my taste for pictorial splendour and to content myself with semi-permanent scenic backgrounds and an emphasis on pace and speed whose value I had learned from Harcourt Williams and the Granville-Barker prefaces. In my youthful enthusiasm I made many mistakes – as a director, of course, I was still a novice – and, looking back over the years, I know that I often achieved less successful results the second time, just as I was inclined to elaborate my own performances from my first sketched essays at the Vic. The Motleys were always admirable colleagues, excelling in their use of inexpensive and innovative materials for costumes (though they looked as expensive as real ones); and we tried to simplify scene changes as much as possible, and to create a fine, if fairly modest, grandeur.

After our successful partnership in the *Romeo and Juliet* of 1935, Olivier and I were destined never to work again together on the stage. I had rather hoped he would ask me to play the Chorus in his film of *Henry V*, but was too proud to suggest it myself. No doubt he feared I should be likely to show off my verse-speaking again at his expense, and he chose Leslie Banks instead.

There was once some talk of our acting together in Anouilh's play *The Rehearsal* when it was to be transferred from Bristol; but the idea was to do it at the Court and I demurred, thinking a bigger West End theatre would be more suitable, and finally neither of us appeared in it. And when I was engaged by him for three plays at the National many years later, and Ibsen's *The Pretenders* was to be staged as the third play, Olivier became too ill to undertake it and the project was abandoned. Peter Shaffer's *Battle of Shrivings* was originally written for us to appear in it together, but again Larry was not well enough, and I was not at all happy when I subsequently played in it myself.

However, my few days as Clarence in his *Richard III* film were extremely pleasant ones, and I have very happy memories of them. Larry, repeating his wonderful stage performance, was at the top of his form, surrounded by old friends, Richardson, myself and Cedric Hardwicke, Michael Gough, and many others – though I was naturally rather upset when my long speech, in the dream scene, before Clarence is murdered, was cut in half to shorten the running time when the film was shown in America.

I did play Joseph Surface to his Sir Peter Teazle (with him and Vivien Leigh) for a charity performance of the screen scene from *The School for Scandal;* and in Tony Palmer's *Wagner* film, Olivier, Richardson, and I were engaged to appear together in one short episode. Much was made of our being reunited after so many years, but it was not a satisfactory scene as written (I had some more effective ones with Richard Burton). We spent a long day in the Hofburg Palace on a freezingly cold day, with all the windows open to let in the lighting cables. During the lunch hour we hid from an eager lady interviewer sent over by the *Daily Mail.* She had expected to lunch with us, but we were not to be prised from the small ante-room where we were surreptitiously wolfing down our sandwiches over a small electric fire. Not unnaturally, the lady was very cross, and wrote a disagreeable account of her visit, saying we were all three completely gaga and could not even remember our lines.

In my *Hamlet* production in London in 1934 the permanent set was built on a turntable which allowed for considerable variation of acting space; but there were too many steps, and we could not manage to turn the big rostrum mechanically without the manual help of stagehands, which meant that we had to lower the curtain continually. In the London *Romeo,* though we solved the problem of lowering the curtain, we found the black velvet cyclorama too gloomy for Verona and replaced it with a blue one after the first night. In both *The Merchant of Venice* and *Richard II* I would have done much better to repeat the very simple decor I had used at the Old Vic and at Oxford, though of course the *Merchant* costumes were in correct period in my later version. But James Agate complained that there were too many candles in the Morocco casket scene (he remarked that the scene itself bored him so much that he decided to count the candles). Similarly, the Oxford production of *Richard* had been extremely simple, with a throne dead centre which remained throughout, and a wall behind it to serve for Flint Castle. The effect was finally far better for the play than the London scenery, which involved elaborate details which I had insisted on (hoping to give the Motleys greater scope) but which cluttered the stage unnecessarily.

Richard II is something of a plaster saint and knows it only too well. But it is a rewarding part, with lovely things to say, and I thought it suited my personality. I had always had a feeling I could do something with the part after I had seen it at the Old Vic with Ernest Milton and, in a Sunday night performance, with Leslie Faber. Unfortunately the character has no humour, and in the beginning the scenes are so very lightly drawn that there isn't much for the King to do in the early part of the play except to sit about in a crown and look decorative. Richard, of course, behaves monstrously at Gaunt's death, but the character does not really come to life until he returns for the great scenes in Wales.

I should really have played Shakespeare's *Richard II* for matinees and *Richard of Bordeaux* on the same evening. I did venture to suggest the idea at the time, because I was so very full of energy in those days. But I remember Francis Lister, who played in *Bordeaux*, saying, 'Oh my God, you do like work, don't you?' It was a great opportunity missed; and the two plays would have made a most effective contrast.

The first time I directed *Richard II* was in 1936 for the OUDS (again at Oxford), where I had worked as director of *Romeo and Juliet* for the first time four years before. Vivien Leigh was guest star this time; and although the Queen is a poor part, she managed to embellish it with her beauty and grace. The Duchess of Gloucester has only one short scene, and I suggested for the part Florence Kahn, a striking looking actress who had made a reputation in America for playing Ibsen before she married Max Beerbohm in 1910. I knew they were living in England at the time, and I thought that, if I persuaded Miss Kahn to play the Duchess, how splendid it would be if Beerbohm could be persuaded to come down and make a speech at the OUDS dinner at the end of the run. Both my invitations were accepted, and I called one morning at the Randolph Hotel to escort the Beerbohms to the first rehearsal. The lady was dressed rather formidably in black, but Beerbohm descended the stairs in a light summer suit and wearing a buttonhole, looking every bit the Edwardian dandy of *Zuleika Dobson* days. (I am not sure whether he wore a straw boater too, but I seem to remember that he did).

On our arrival at the theatre, Beerbohm buried himself in an empty stall, while Miss Kahn came up onto the stage, where I began rather timidly to direct her scene. Her partner was a very shy undergraduate, much shorter than she was and extremely nervous. As we proceeded, she alarmed him by waving her right arm at intervals, motioning him imperiously downstage so that she could command the best position for herself. Needless to say, this traditional actor-manager behaviour completely destroyed the confidence of poor John of Gaunt. However, Miss Kahn appeared to relax at the OUDS dinner, even coyly putting a flower in her hair, which she plucked from the vase on the table in front of her. 'The Incomparable Max' obliged in his best manner with a delightful speech.

*

Today, *King Lear* is far more familiar to the public than it used to be, owing to a number of productions in recent years, as well as to several television versions. (Karen Blixen used to say that she knew the play by heart, and would judge a man only by whether he knew every word of it). Granville-Barker once told me that the King should be witty and sly as well as wicked and mad. Lear and Hamlet both have a good deal of humour, as he pointed out, which is a great help in trying to act them, whereas there is no humour whatever in either Macbeth or Othello. Many Lears have tried to rationalise the coming madness by making him also senile, showing an unhinged mind from the very start, but I think that the first scene should be simple and majestic. For all the rash things he does, Lear has complete control at first, though he does uncontrollable things which he later will come to regret.

I was once talking to Edith Sitwell about the play and we discussed three interesting details in it. One was the conviction I have always had that Cordelia and the Fool must originally have been played by the same boy actor. Cordelia appears in the opening scene of the play, and then it is nearly two hours before we see her again. In the scene directly after Lear has renounced her, the character of the Fool is suddenly introduced and is continually reminding him of Cordelia. The Fool dies, rather arbitrarily, at the end of the storm scenes in the hut, and immediately afterwards Cordelia returns. Then, in the scene of her death, when Lear says, 'My poor fool is hang'd', an Elizabethan audience, knowing the Fool was the same actor, would have found this reference very much more moving.

Edith Sitwell told me that when Lear rushes from the castle calling for his troop of horse and disappearing into the night, it is exactly what Henry VIII did when he heard of the adultery of Catherine Howard. The King disappeared for about two weeks and nobody knew where he had gone. This episode must have been talked of in London, and perhaps it was known to Shakespeare.

Then there is a very strange line in the scene on Dover Cliff (Act 4, Scene VI) between Gloucester and Lear, in which the old king says 'It were a delicate stratagem to shoe a troop of horse with felt.' Edith Sitwell said that at the Field of Cloth of Gold in France, where enormous tents were built for the meeting of Francis I and Henry VIII, the champions rode in to the banquet and the hooves of their horses were shod with felt so that they would not slip on the specially laid marble pavements. Shakespeare might well have heard about this, too.

One cannot help wondering, in these days when we have instantaneous communication with people on the other side of the world, how topical news was spread throughout Elizabethan England, whether by rumour, messenger, or legend. There are famous references to contemporary events in *A Midsummer Night's Dream, Julius Caesar,* and *Henry V,* and I have even heard it suggested that the murder of Darnley with the connivance of Mary Stuart has echoes in the plots of both *Hamlet* and *Macbeth.* The character of Lear would surely have been easily accepted by an Elizabethan audience, some of whom would remember Henry VIII, dead some 60 years before, with his extraordinary mixture of power, cruelty, and charm.

Someone said that Granville-Barker had spoilt my entrance in *Lear* when I came on downstage from the side and walked up to the throne with my back to the audience. He placed the throne dead centre, with three seats on each side of it carefully allotted to the principal characters, and the whole scene was arranged in a formal symmetrical way. 'Do not listen to people who say that the first act is impossible,' Granville-Barker said. 'It is just like the Old Testament or one of the great fairy stories: *"there was once an old king with three daughters . . ."*.'

We had a very fine cast for this production, which was staged for only a few weeks at the Vic at the time of the fall of France in 1940. Fay Compton played Regan as a cold pussy cat, with Granville-Barker's help. I remember that in a short scene with Oswald, after the death of Cornwall, he had her making up, with a mirror in her hand, dressed in widow's weeds.

I wonder whether Goneril was played as being pregnant in Shakespeare's day. We never made a point of that in any of the productions I was in, but I think it should be rather important to emphasise Lear's great curse (Act I, Scene IV). I was puzzled by the fact that the King leaves the stage immediately after that speech. Almost at once he returns, attacks her again in another speech, and then rushes out of the castle. I said to Granville-Barker, 'He comes back shouting that his followers have been suddenly dismissed without his knowledge. How could he know that? Who told him off-stage?' Granville-Barker said it didn't matter, that until Pinero and Ibsen, playwrights did not bother to account for off-stage time. They knew the audience would accept that an actor went off the stage to write a letter and that when he came back the letter was written, whereas Pinero and Ibsen allowed the exact time which would elapse before he returned.

He told me, too, that the most important thing in the mad scenes of *Lear* was to keep the progression right. The other short intervening scenes, with Edmund and Gloucester, break up the big storm scenes, and Lear must come back on the verge of the same point of madness as when he left the stage, to show that his mental decay is gradually working towards his complete breakdown. Granville-Barker's notes on the mad scenes in *Lear* were wonderfully illuminating. The few passages he showed me himself as we rehearsed were wonderful, and I always tried to observe them when I played the part again. He demanded lightness at Dover Cliff, and again lightness ('like a polka') in 'Come let's away to prison' with Cordelia in Act 5, Scene III. He said the king should shrivel into a timid wisp of a man after he finally goes mad – he should suddenly diminish before one's eyes.

No acting can ever be completely naturalistic, and I suppose what impresses an audience most is if an actor can do something very natural in the climax of a Shakespeare part, but on a different scale. This must have been partly, I think, the secret of Ellen Terry's enormous popularity (quite apart from her talent). She could suddenly drop – just as Shakespeare does – from a very high style of speech and manner into something so simple and human that the whole audience was immediately touched by it. When Shakespeare says: 'Dost thou not see my baby at my breast that sucks the nurse asleep?' or 'All the perfumes of Arabia will not sweeten this little hand', or 'Pray you undo this button', there is something so infinitely touching about these lines that, if they come at the right drop of temperature from the big noble scaffolding which supports them, they can have the most superb effect on the stage.

One of the great difficulties in staging *Lear* is how to convey the impression of the storm. I always had to compete with a contrived background and knew I would not be able to dominate it. Strikingly realistic sound effects are possible now – but they do not seem to be any more convincing in the theatre than the old ones. The storm that for me succeeded best was the one Peter Brook created with a few ropes for his production of *The Tempest* in 1957. I suppose that in Shakespeare's day they just fired a few cannons to add to a lot of rumblings behind the scenes. It might be interesting to see the *Lear* storm scenes played without any sound effects at all. Komisarjevsky once did the play at Oxford with the undergraduates and achieved a splendid production, which he repeated later at Stratford (with Randle Ayrton as the King). He had some kind of harmonium or Hammond organ playing behind the scenes with the stop pulled out, making a continuous kind of hum, but nothing more, with strikingly good results. Maybe one should aim for an effect not like real thunder and lightning, but for something equally disruptive and creepy; and with our modern switchboards the lights can, of course, do wonders.

I would love to have been directed in *Lear* by Peter Brook, but he wanted a more craggy personality and chose Paul Scofield. When Scofield fell ill and the opening had to be postponed, I offered to fill the breach, but Peter would not have me and I was rather disappointed. His production was very fine, I thought, except that he cut out the sympathetic bits with the servants after Gloucester's blinding, and he rather underplayed all the Cordelia scenes. Perhaps he was afraid of being thought sentimental. But there *is* a simple kind of English pathos in certain scenes of Shakespeare which must be handled so cunningly by the director and the actors that they do not seem sentimental at all. The fact that Brook is not completely English may have something to do with his treatment of such scenes, although his cosmopolitan background has probably greatly contributed to his unique genius.

I no longer feel tempted to play Lear on the screen, since I no longer have the voice or the staying power. Olivier looked me straight in the eye a few years ago and said, 'Johnny, you don't want to play Lear again, do you?' I said, 'Well, I don't know.' Of course he lived to be able to carry out his wish, a most gallantly typical example of his most extraordinary determination and resilience. But I think *Lear* is an impossible play to screen unless one can devise a superb new idea of how to adapt it. Of course, the part really needs a bass voice. Olivier used to say to me that he and I were both very lucky to have been able to play three great parts that are written for basses – Macbeth, Othello and Lear – while we were both tenors. I think that is true. Many people think that, because he had such great vocal qualities, Frederick Valk was the greatest Lear of recent times, but was not appreciated at the time because of his accent.

Many people think that Wolfit's Lear was wonderful, too; but I never saw him in the part.

I used to tell Ralph Richardson he ought to play Lear, but he would say, 'Oh no, it's a romantic part – it's better for you.' And I thought to myself, 'Well, if I've made it into a romantic part, I'm not at all sure that it's written that way.' I think he was only paying me a compliment. He ought to have been wonderful as Lear, for he had so many of the essential qualities but, oddly enough, when he came to play Othello and Macbeth he was never happy in either part, while as Enobarbus, Kent and Caliban, in those two seasons with me at the Old Vic in 1930, he was superb. He was certainly the definitive Falstaff and he was a fine Iago, too.

CHAPTER THREE

MACBETH

MICHAEL AYRTON, who designed my *Macbeth* in 1942, was an obstinate, quarrelsome, talented young artist, who fought me doggedly whenever I criticised his work. (I once took him to meet Kenneth Clark at the National Gallery, but he seemed to think little of the drawings Ayrton showed him.) John Minton, on the other hand, with his long beautiful Modigliani face, was wonderfully agreeable and sympathetic in designing the costumes and was deservedly popular with all of us; sadly, he was destined to commit suicide not long afterwards. Ayrton's scenery was marbled, chequered and striped. There were huge hands and strange crowns hung in odd places, which were tiresomely intrusive.

The play is awkward scenically. In the first act there are eight short scenes, varying from the heath to the much more intimate episode of Lady Macbeth reading the letter, as well as the short scene in Duncan's court followed by the murder scene in the castle courtyard. It is extremely difficult to decide how to space out the stage so as to use it satisfactorily to suggest all these backgrounds. Gordon Craig's screens, moving in and out silently, which he planned for his Stanislavsky *Hamlet*, might, I think, have provided a fine solution to the problem, but war conditions, and the fact that he never lived in England, made me too wary of approaching him as I might otherwise have done.

Ayrton may have been influenced by Pavel Tchelitcheff, who had made a great success in Paris with his scenery for *Ondine,* staged by Louis Jouvet. I never saw it, but the photographs I saw looked very effective, and I asked my Mother, who was a severe critic and happened to be in Paris, to write to me about it. She had not been impressed: 'There were real fountains on the stage', she remarked, 'but I saw equally good ones years ago in Augustus Harris's pantomimes at Drury Lane!'

I treated the whole play too romantically, as well as being too romantic myself for the part of Macbeth. When I had first played the part at the Vic with Harcourt Williams I had had no time to study it very deeply. I copied from an old souvenir drawing of Irving's production the idea of Macbeth entering with a sheathed sword on my shoulder, and I did quite a lot of things that I had read Irving did. He was always a great idol of mine, although I never saw him act – he died the year after I was born. But from what I had read about him I thought that if he had managed to succeed with Hamlet, Macbeth, and Benedick, in none of which characters he was particularly well cast (and obviously hampered by his awkward mannerisms of speech and gait), perhaps I might dare to take the plunge myself. I think Ellen Terry's description of Irving as 'a gaunt famished wolf' is a wonderful picture of what Macbeth should be in the last act.

The finest Macbeth I have ever seen was Laurence Olivier's, when he played the part at Stratford. He came on as a black soul, showing that he had the idea of murder in his mind, whether he knew it or not, even before he met the witches or came back to his wife, though I had always read the text quite differently.

Macbeth is one of my favourite plays, but it is a famously unlucky one. When I directed it with Ralph Richardson at Stratford in the 1950s it was a great failure. I rashly designed the scenery myself, which was all black (and I was rather proud of it) but most people thought the idea very obvious. I thought I had managed the apparitions and the battle, with Birnam Wood advancing, rather well; but it was no use. And though Margaret Leighton was very good, Richardson was unhappy. He kept on saying, 'Well, if *I* can't see the dagger, cocky, do you wonder the audience can't, either?' Which was very endearing, but it did not help his performance.

I once begged Edith Evans to play Lady Macbeth but she firmly refused. She said a part of the character was missing; there was nothing between her collapse after the murder scene and the sleep-walking scene to show that she is going out of her mind. It is often said that the part is almost impossible for an actress to succeed in (despite the legend of Mrs Siddons), and I have seldom seen anybody (until Judi Dench) satisfy me in the part. Judith Anderson was curiously ineffective. When she played it at the Vic in London with Olivier she was not thought by the critics here to be very interesting, although she made an enormous success in it later with Maurice Evans in America. Vivien Leigh's performance at Stratford was, I think, almost the best thing I ever saw her do – but on a small scale. It was a great regret to me, as well as for Olivier and herself, that the money could not be found to make the film. I think that her performance, if it had been transferred to the screen, would have been enormously effective. Gwen Ffrangcon-Davies, in my 1942 production, was also blamed by the critics for being too fragile and feminine. I thought her brilliant, but she had to contend with too much scenery and – except for Leon Quartermaine, who was a splendid Banquo (even as a Ghost in the banquet scene) – an inadequate supporting cast.

Certainly *Macbeth* is an unlucky play. We had a terrible time with this wartime production of it. Several people died during the long provincial tour. One dear old Cornish actress, who was by far the best of the witches, became ill, but she insisted on sitting in the wings of the cold Scala Theatre in London, wrapped in shawls, while we rehearsed. She suddenly arrived at the Midland Hotel in Manchester in a hired car, saying she must be near the theatre, where we were keeping the part open for her with her understudy. She ordered dinner in bed, asked Hugh Beaumont to come up to talk to her, and had her hair cut. In the morning the manager rang to tell me she had died during the night, while we had been engaged in a dress rehearsal lasting till four o'clock in the morning. A fine actor, Marcus Barron, who played Duncan, died some weeks later; Macduff had to be replaced; and when we at last arrived in London, Gwen Ffrangcon-Davies walked into a lamp post in the black-out and got a bruised eye.

For the six months before our West End opening we had played fortnightly runs all over England, and in each theatre I had to re-light the play all through every Sunday, because there were different switchboards in every city. The Blackpool theatre was enormous and we did not do at all well there. When we played in Edinburgh, pupils from two very grand schools came to a matinee and they giggled in the wrong places and showered paper cups from the dress circle to the stalls. I was determined not to interrupt the performance, so I just kept making Macready pauses and frowning at the audience. The children did not seem to find amusement in the witches or apparitions, but when I came on to greet my wife, in the first scene where we meet, they shrieked with laughter when I kissed her. The following week, at a public lunch in Edinburgh, I was asked to make a speech, and in the course of it remarked that I had been puzzled by the fact that when I entered and kissed my wife, the audience seemed to think this the funniest thing in the play. Next day a letter appeared in *The Scotsman* saying, 'We do understand Mr Gielgud's feelings, but perhaps he did not realise that husbands and wives in Scotland do not kiss at breakfast-time!'

The imaginative side of Macbeth has always appealed to me. Though I knew I would never be able to do justice to the warrior, there is also a romantic and visionary quality in him, and a kind of weakness that his wife brings out so clearly. I saw the part in the opposite way to Olivier. I thought that when Macbeth first comes on he should seem to be what everyone says he is in the first two scenes: the great warrior chieftain who is Duncan's greatest general and, having won this battle nobly for him, comes back flushed with success. Then when he meets the witches and comes home to his wife, these two influences, at such a critical moment in his career, suddenly topple him from his height. And yet Olivier convinced me absolutely in his performance; so, too, did Ian McKellen in the Royal Shakespeare Company production of 1977, when Trevor Nunn directed the play so brilliantly at the Donmar Warehouse with no scenery at all. This made it much easier not to have to stage an elaborate banquet scene and cope with period costumes. Everything was simplified to feed the play. Both McKellen and Judi Dench brought it off to perfection I thought, and of course it was quite a new experience to see the play in such a very small theatre. We were close to the actors, and the text came over marvellously. One of the most effective things was the moment when lights were thrown up from behind us in the audience to give a feeling of outdoors when, after the banquet scene, the Macbeths rose to leave their thrones. All the cast sat on boxes around the stage and walked into the acting area when necessary. I liked everything except the men's costumes. I couldn't think why the courtiers were dressed in pinstriped trousers and butterfly collars when Duncan himself had a beautiful white robe, and Malcolm's white sweater suddenly made one think inevitably of Lillywhite's.

It seems impossible to stage *Macbeth* in any kind of realistic or spectacular way. I saw Sybil Thorndike and Henry Ainley in a production by Lewis Casson, for which Charles Ricketts had designed the scenery and costumes, which was very ambitious. But there were mimed tableaux of the battle scenes which did not work at all, and the play became so slow, what with intervals and music, that it hung fire all the time.

CHAPTER FOUR

The Merchant of Venice • Measure for Measure • Twelfth Night • Much Ado About Nothing • A Midsummer Night's Dream

GRANVILLE-BARKER said *The Merchant of Venice* was a fairy story. I had acted the part of Shylock at my prep school, even though only in the trial scene. Then I played Antonio when *The Merchant* was the second production at the Vic in my first season there in 1929. It is rather an ungrateful part, and I was already longing to attempt Shylock – the more so when I happened to catch Brember Wills, who was rehearsing the part very ineffectively and with whom I shared a dressing-room, busily perusing a Christian Science manual, which maintained that all hatred was a sin. (Wills was an excellent actor – though not at his best in Shakespeare – and was the original Shotover in the first London production of *Heartbreak House*.)

When *The Merchant* was to be done at the Vic again in 1932, and I was no longer in the company, I offered to come and direct it myself, having already directed *Romeo and Juliet* at Oxford for the OUDS. This Oxford experiment had encouraged me greatly, and I was longing to embark on further experiments. I devised a very simple production for this Old Vic *Merchant*, a permanent set – mostly in hessian – and a medley of costumes of mixed periods, beautifully designed at minimum cost by Motley, who had worked with me at Oxford, and would later create the decor for *Richard of Bordeaux, Hamlet,* and *Romeo and Juliet,* as well as for Rodney Ackland's *The Old Ladies* and André Obey's *Noah.*

The Vic *Merchant* was put on with only about ten days' rehearsal, but it came out remarkably well. I was acting in the West End at the same time, and Harcourt Williams took over from me once or twice. I rewarded him by remarking in my first-night speech that I owed much to Harcourt Williams who had done all the donkey work! I used a great deal of music – Peter Warlock's *Capriole Suite* (on records of course: the Vic could not run to a live orchestra), and Peggy Ashcroft delighted me with her Portia, a part she was to play many times in subsequent years. Malcolm Keen was a disappointing Shylock, but the lightness and charm of the play succeeded surprisingly well – though, because I was acting every evening, I never saw it with an audience. But I was much gratified to receive an enthusiastic letter from Tyrone Guthrie, who was already one of the best directors in the country.

When I finally came to play Shylock in 1937, I tried to make him a squalid little guttersnipe. This was not much liked by the public or the critics, and I did not satisfy myself in it either. Of course, it was the time of Hitler, which did not help matters. Perhaps I would have satisfied more people if I had created a haughty Irvingesque character rather than a cringing Fagin-figure – though Olivier told me he liked me in it better than almost anything else I did in Shakespeare. I think I did good work on the play because I loved all the Belmont scenes, which are often considered very silly. I have never found any difficulty in accepting the plots of either *Lear* or *The Merchant of Venice,* though many people think the stories preposterous.

Nowadays it is almost impossible to do *The Merchant* without seeing Shylock's point of view and sympathising with him to some extent. I can't say I approved of Jonathan Miller's conception. I thought it was absurd to set the play in the Edwardian period, when the Jews were so very important and successful in England; I thought it made rather nonsense of the whole structure of the play. Kenneth Tynan described Shylock as a comic monster, a very good description. I would have liked to have been more comic myself. What I lacked was power; certainly most of the critics thought so.

I once said, stupidly, in some interview or other, that I found it practically impossible to be disliked on the stage. But I had no such problem when I came to play Angelo in *Measure for Measure*. I did not have to worry whether he was sympathetic or not: he cannot be anything but a despicable character. Peter Brook directed the last act, in which Angelo is humbled, with tremendously telling pauses – enormously effective for my speeches of repentance. I had seen the play some twenty years before at the Old Vic, when Charles Laughton played Angelo and was wonderfully wicked and lecherous, prowling up and down the stage in a big black cloak. I thought I could perhaps do something with Angelo, and when I was asked to go to Stratford in 1950 I rather casually accepted it as the opening play. I had never worked with Peter Brook before. We took to each other immediately, and I put myself entirely in his hands. It was a great milestone in the second half of my career.

Because of the name of Angelo, I though he was probably very good looking, so I ordered a flaxen wig down to my shoulders and a beautiful grey velvet robe. When I came on at the dress rehearsal they all said from the front, 'How splendid you look, about 25, so young and elegant,' and I blushed and smirked. There was a long pause and then Brook said '. . . but it doesn't have anything to do with your performance. You must change it completely.' So, between the dress rehearsal and the first night, I abolished the wig in favour of a close-fitting cap and a severe serge robe. Evidently my performance had been sufficiently right in rehearsal for both Brook and myself to realise that the clothes and wig had been absolutely wrong.

I remember experiencing, when I went on for the first night, the kind of relaxed feeling which I had sought, without knowing it, for so many years. I first became aware of it at the very beginning of my career when I had played Trofimov in *The Cherry Orchard* at Oxford with Fagan; I remember coming on to the stage on that first night wearing a bald wig and spectacles and using a rather shambling gait, and I suddenly felt I was not an actor showing off but a student living in a real family; it was more like being part of a novel than acting in a play. In those early years I was very highly strung and thought that if I was intense enough the audience would respond, whereas actually I was putting them against me, because I worked too hard and exhausted them as well as myself.

In *Measure for Measure* Peter Brook created a menacing atmosphere like a Breughel, with arches and a great deal of dark costuming, and he lit much of the action by torchlight, which was enormously effective. We were allowed to use flaming torches at Stratford, but the LCC banned them in London when I tried to use them in my *Romeo* production in 1935, and I was forced to use lanterns, which were not nearly so effective.

I think what I first understood about Angelo (perhaps because I found something of it in myself) was that he is deeply repressed, and when he realises that he hopes to seduce Isabella it really shocks him deeply and he does everything to cover it up. Yvonne Mitchell very generously said that when I touched Isabella on the arm it was obvious that I had an orgasm at the same time! If that was really the effect I made, it could only have been because I was thinking the part the right way.

I think *Twelfth Night* is one of the most difficult plays for the director as well as for the actors, and I have never seen a completely satisfactory version of it. It is said that Granville-Barker's production at the Savoy in 1912 was superb. I failed when I directed it with the Oliviers at Stratford in 1955 under what should have been very happy conditions. The cast was very good and included a number of my colleagues from other plays. But the theatre itself was rather against me. It is a very difficult house for directing comedy because it is so badly shaped. Then I found Olivier was not very well-disposed towards my ideas. He had his own conception of the character, and gave it a funny accent (and a funny nose) and I had the feeling that he probably re-directed Vivien Leigh as Viola after I had finished rehearsing with her.

I had seen two or three productions of the play by Tyrone Guthrie in which the cruel part of the action was very much emphasised and the Malvolio plot very malicious, with his mad scene rather brutal at the end. The better Malvolio is played the more difficult it is to harmonise his character with the rest of the play. The best performance I have ever seen was given by Richard Briers, who played it quite recently at the Riverside in a very striking production by Kenneth Branagh, and combined the comic and tragic sides of the character extremely well.

This was one of the few productions of Shakespeare that I have seen from the front in recent years. At first I found it very hard to accept the permanent setting of a snowbound garden, but the actors, though not outstandingly good for the most part, achieved a remarkably charming romantic ensemble which served the play in the end extremely well, though I was very much annoyed by the second scene of the play being put first, and I found the class distinctions, so important in the action, were not sufficiently observed. Orsino had to sit in civilian clothes on an armchair planted in the snow, and I ventured to suggest to Branagh that if he had been dressed in furs, with a peaked cap with a coronet round it, like the picture of Ludwig of Bavaria driving in his sledge, the effect would have been justifiably more romantic.

Viola and Olivia are very difficult parts. Peggy Ashcroft was a wonderful Viola, but I never thought she had a production worthy of her performance. I saw a production by Fagan at the Royal Court years ago with a wonderful Sir Toby (Arthur Whitby from the Granville-Barker era); also a rather good performance in Paris, beautifully acted, with Suzanne Flon, who played Viola enchantingly, and an excellent Malvolio. One very funny invention was in the letter scene, when the comics had little model trees, which they carried round with them and hid behind when necessary, while Malvolio kept on turning round and wondering how the trees could possibly have moved to a different place.

I played Malvolio only once myself, at the opening of Sadler's Wells in 1931, in a very poor production, though Ralph Richardson was a splendid Toby Belch. It was a tremendously over-publicised occasion of which we were all very much aware. We didn't think we did justice to the play, and Sadler's Wells was a very difficult theatre (as difficult as Stratford) to play comedy in because it has so little contact with the audience: no boxes and a very recessed stage. Harcourt Williams tried to solve the problem by building two stone staircases coming out of the orchestra pit, which we used a great deal, and which helped to push the action a bit farther forward. But it was never a happy theatre in which to play Shakespeare. After I left, the company went back to the Vic again, and were much happier there.

I always had an idea I wanted to do *Much Ado About Nothing*, partly I think because Ellen Terry and Irving had made such a success of it. I did a few scenes from it at drama school, playing Benedick, only to discover that I didn't find the speeches and situations the least funny. But when at last I came to direct it at Stratford I fell in love with the play. The production lasted me nearly ten years. I played Benedick with three different Beatrices – Diana Wynyard, Peggy Ashcroft and Margaret

Leighton – and different casts from 1950 to 1959, when I took it to America with the basis of the same production. But by this time the spontaneity seemed to have gone out of it and my ideas were tired. The whole thing became rather a travesty of the very successful production it was when I had first directed it in 1949. Then, Anthony Quayle and Diana Wynyard played Benedick and Beatrice and I was not acting in it myself. Having seen it from the front with their very good performances one year, and then played Benedick myself the next, with Peggy as Beatrice, I gained a great knowledge of the play, and I felt we really brought out the spirit of it very successfully.

In the part of Benedick I kept on trying to make myself more of the soldier. In the beginning the designer Mariano Andreu gave me comic hats to wear, one like a blancmange and another like a cartwheel with feathers. These used to get laughs as soon as I came on in them, and I decided this was a bit cheap, and bit by bit I modified the hats and added leather doublets and top boots.

I had seen the play only once before I tackled it myself, when my uncle Fred Terry played Benedick; but by then he was too old for it, and he did farcical things like hiding in a tree in the orchard scene and falling out of it. He was now very fat and more like Falstaff (which he would have played superbly), though he was fine in the church, as he always was when he played love scenes.

When Peggy Ashcroft first came to rehearsal she approached the part of Beatrice quite differently from Diana Wynyard, and kept on opposing me over things that I suggested. I kept on wondering whether she was right, but I trusted her extraordinary instinct for knowing what she could do and what didn't suit her in Diana's style (her elaborate costumes for instance), and I found many interesting new colours in my partnership with her. We had played *Romeo and Juliet* together in the Thirties, but had appeared together only once in comedy, when she played Cecily most beautifully in *The Importance of Being Earnest*. Fortunately Diana Wynyard was one of her greatest friends, so there was no envy between them or resentment from Peggy at being asked to follow her in the part.

Oberon is one of the few fine parts in Shakespeare that is not a great physical strain. I always thought I had been rather good as Oberon at the Vic, but when I played it again at the Haymarket in 1944 I was very bad indeed. Neither Peggy or I were as good as we had hoped to be. We both felt we were too old for the parts by then and could no longer feel the freshness of the play. Also the production (by Nevill Coghill) was rather disappointing. I had suggested *A Midsummer Night's Dream* with great enthusiasm, but the moment we began to rehearse I saw that it was not a good play for our company, which was distinctly middle-aged.

The limelight is easily stolen by Bottom, and the comics always go wonderfully in the last act. But funnily enough, though I loved the brilliantly inventive Stratford production by Peter Brook with the white box, I did not very much care for the Pyramus and Thisbe scene, which is usually absolutely foolproof and has succeeded in every other production I have seen. Nor did I feel happy about Bottom being translated without his ass's head, or Puck coming down into the audience.

The great difficulty in *The Dream* is the fairies. I remember Granville-Barker's famous 1914 production which, although I was only ten years old, I was lucky enough to see, and I was enormously impressed with the gold fairies. There were conventional Greek costumes for the mortals as far as I remember. But Basil Dean staged a very heavy production at Drury Lane in the early Twenties with Edith Evans, Athene Seyler, Gwen Ffrangcon-Davies and a very starry cast, and with huge sets by George Harris, who was Dean's favourite designer and extremely talented. But the forest scene looked like a camouflaged tank stranded on a huge slope, with everyone running up and down, and the Mendelssohn music was played in full, slowing up the action.

I greatly admired Brook's invention – the originality and freshness of the whole attack, the coils of wire, and the lack of any old-fashioned gauzy prettiness. Though I don't remember his production in great detail, the effect of the whole was wonderfully striking. But I gather it depended greatly on the quality of each performance, which seemed to vary from day to day. Friends of mine who were with me in New York when it was produced there, went on the first night and came back ravished by it. But they went again a week later and were terribly disappointed; they thought it had been spoiled because it was such a big success. 'Something seems to have happened to the production,' they said, 'perhaps because it's supposed to be so marvellous. The actors have lost confidence in some way.'

I suppose that is true of a great deal of acting. One wishes people hadn't seen it on that particular night. When I was playing Hamlet for the last time in 1944, I was frightfully tired at the end of the war, and I used to think: 'Twice today I've got to play Hamlet, this great part that I shall never play again. And I can't do it today. I could do it tomorrow, or next week, but I can't do it now.' Being forced to carry out a job is part of our discipline as actors, but it must affect performances and productions far more than people imagine. Of course, the whole experience of going to the theatre today is so very different from what it was in my young days. Then it was the first night that was all-important, even though there were often disasters – people drying up, scenery sticking, endless waits. And then, too, the press notices all came out the very next day. I was very glad, when I played Lear at Stratford in 1950 and the first night was not as successful as I had hoped, that T.C. Worsley, the theatre critic of the *New Statesman*, took the trouble to go again on the second night and said that my performance was so very much better. One is always to some extent a victim of one's health, of the audience, of the other actors, of the director, of the atmosphere in front.

Films are quite different, because they are hardly ever shot in sequence, and you don't have to repeat them eight times a week. A scene can be repeated until actors and director are satisfied. I think this is one of the reasons why Edith Evans was happier on the screen at the end of her great career. She could no longer bear the discipline of having to create a performance absolutely at the moment, though she had been used to doing so all her life. In the theatre, any small change in the performances of the actors around her would immediately distract and put her off, but when filming she seemed not to be disturbed by the closeness of the technicians and the cameras or the lack of a theatre audience, and could be certain of the opportunity of another take if she felt she could improve her performance in any way.

CHAPTER FIVE

Julius Caesar • *Othello* • Wolsey in *Henry VIII* • *Chimes at Midnight*

I HAVE played Julius Caesar on the stage as well as in a film version, but Caesar is not really very interesting: Cassius is the part. I once played Mark Antony years ago at The Vic, and I always rather wanted to play Brutus, a very difficult character and also, surely, Shakespeare's first sketch for Hamlet and Macbeth. Hugh Beaumont and I talked of doing the play in London in the early Seventies, but I felt we could not stage it without a big crowd, and he could not afford the sort of crowd that would have been possible in the Edwardian theatre. When I suggested to John Schlesinger that I play Julius Caesar myself at the National Theatre I thought they would be able to have a wonderful crowd in the huge Olivier theatre, but in the end there were only about twenty people, and I was very disappointed in the result.

The only time I have seen a really wonderful crowd was at the famous Gala Tercentenary performance at Drury Lane in 1916, when stars like Gerald du Maurier and Edmund Gwenn played the First and Second Citizens, and the forum scene was directed by Granville-Barker. Beerbohm Tree's Edwardian productions (for which he could engage a lot of soldiers for a shilling a night) had always been considered very spectacular, but they seem to have been rather cobbled together. Bernard

Shaw described how, in Tree's *Caesar* production, in spite of all the lavish pictorial Alma Tadema scenery, the cloths flapped about and the soldiers returned from the battle with weapons obviously unused. But in the 1916 Gala production, for just that one afternoon, the forum scene was tremendously effective, with Henry Ainley as a splendid Antony. I have never again seen the play staged with a big crowd.

The performance which impressed me most at Drury Lane on that occasion was that of H.B. Irving, who played Cassius, and when I went to Stratford in 1950 and got the chance of playing the part myself I leapt at the opportunity. I was not at all happy at rehearsals. But Anthony Quayle, who was directing and playing Antony, said 'Think of all those men with medals and bowler hats in Whitehall who are dissatisfied and bitter because they haven't got the gongs they think they deserve to have.' To my great surprise I had a success on the first night, when I just rushed at it like a bull at a gate. It is always a great question in *Julius Caesar* how the three leading parts are to be balanced so as to make an effective contrast. It would be interesting to have them alternated by three fine actors – as the Booth brothers, I believe, once did in New York.

I have never seen *Caesar* played in Elizabethan dress, but of course there are many references in the play to an Elizabethan background – doublets, clocks and all sorts of anachronisms. It is supposed to be difficult for most actors to feel at ease in togas, whereas Elizabethan dress can be very appropriate to all the plays. Orson Welles' production in America in 1937 was played in black shirts and uniforms *à la* Mussolini and created much excitement at the time; but I thought our modern uniforms at the National were a great mistake, since the early scenes of the play should emphasize a civilian murder in the domestic environment of a city, in deliberate contrast to the later battle scenes.

When I acted in the film of *Julius Caesar*, having played

Cassius on the stage only a year before, I found I didn't have to change my performance for the screen very much, except to tone it down a bit, and I felt I had more hope of being effective because I knew the shape of it so well. Fortunately, the screenplay was fairly faithful to the original text, and not much was cut. The old actors used to cut and transpose very arbitrarily. I once played the scene of Cassius, Brutus, and Casca, with Godfrey Tearle as Brutus and Claude Rains as Casca, for a gala at Drury Lane. When we came to rehearse I found that Tearle had changed the order of several speeches and made some cuts, too. I asked him why and he explained, 'Oh, my father always did it.' Such can be the dangerous adherence to stage tradition. When Henry Irving's Shylock returned after the elopement of Jessica and knocked at his door as the curtain fell, everyone was struck by the innovation. The Shylocks that came after him attempted to go one better. Beerbohm Tree rushed into the house, put ashes on his head and appeared at the upper window, screaming. But Olivier invented a brilliant touch when he carried on Jessica's dress in the Tubal scene.

The first time I ever saw *Hamlet*, with H.B. Irving, the son of the great Victorian actor, Ophelia (played by Lady Forbes-Robertson) was brought on as a dripping corpse after she was drowned. In the Edwardian theatre they were always very fond of tableaux. But even as late as 1932 I recall seeing a production at His Majesty's of *Julius Caesar* in which, at the end of the murder scene, Calpurnia came back and crouched, mourning, over her husband's body.

When I heard that Alan Ayckbourn had rearranged the order of some scenes in *Othello* I did not like the sound of that at all; and I've already mentioned my disapproval of Kenneth Branagh's transposing of the first two scenes of *Twelfth Night*. I argued with him, saying, 'Irving did the same thing and so did Tree – but how can you not open the play with "Let music be the food of love"?' It's like playing one of Beethoven's third movements first.

Although it is very important for an actor to be ambitious and to want to widen his range, it is just as important for him to know what his physical limitations must forbid him to do. I should never have attempted to play Othello. The critics said I ought to have known I was miscast, but that perhaps I should have played Iago when I was young. In the old days Iago was always acted by a middle-aged leading man, and it was not until the best days of Stratford and the Vic that the directors read the text more carefully and found that Iago was only 28. It would have been a wonderful part to have played when I was a young man, but it would never have occurred to me to choose it in those days, though I did appear in a radio version of the play many years ago with Henry Ainley as Othello.

Ralph Richardson's 1937 Othello was not successful, but in the same production (at the Old Vic) Olivier played Iago and gave one of his most brilliant and witty performances. I have never seen another Iago who is also really funny. I am sure that Shakespeare intends Iago to amuse the audience, especially since Othello (like Macbeth) has no sense of humour.

When Olivier made his great success as Othello I was staggered when he came on in the first scene sniffing a rose. But then I suddenly recalled a remark of Franco Zeffirelli's when we were rehearsing my disastrous Othello at Stratford. He had said: 'I believe this man is very vain.' 'Nonsense,' I had replied, 'he is the great warrior whom everybody respects and admires so much.'

When it was suggested I should play Othello, I thought maybe it was a good idea as I had made quite a success as Leontes. But I have neither the voice nor the power for Othello, and I should never have attempted it. I didn't realise this at the time, thinking that, as with Leontes, it was another play about jealousy. But Leontes' jealousy is so hysterical and paranoid that I somehow found a way to play it. And in that 1951 production I had Peter Brook's invaluable help. He took the play in his stride, and, as there are not a great many traditions attached to it, we both felt able to work along very straightforward lines. I had seen *The Winter's Tale* only once before, at Stratford, and found it a very fascinating play – though I had never been able even to read it before.

With Shakespeare's heroes it is fatal to play too much for sympathy, and whenever I played Hamlet I kept trying to find the unattractive aspect of his character. I used to watch Edith Evans carefully to see how she always tried to find the 'other side' of a part. When I showed her *The Seagull* (after she had played the Nurse in *Romeo and Juliet*), I said, 'I hope you will play Arkadina. Of course, she's rather a bitch'. She looked at me very oddly, and took the play away. The next day she came to me and said, 'I don't think she's a bitch at all.' And I knew then she was going to find the sympathetic side of the character and play it as all apparently unattractive parts must be played. Iago must surely be able to revel in his own wickedness. Even Richard III has to find some sort of justification for himself, for then the character becomes fascinating both for him and for the audience. I am sure that Iago thinks he is right. People ask, 'Why is Iago so wicked?' But surely wicked people are never wicked to themselves? The fascination of Olivier's acting, both as Iago and as Richard III, was to watch him delighting in his own wicked cleverness and sharing his pleasure with the audience.

In 1958 I played Wolsey in *Henry VIII* – rather indifferently, as I always thought. I have never cared greatly for that rather straggling pageant of a play, though Tyrone Guthrie directed some very lively revivals both at Stratford and in London that were marred only by his delight in too much comic business and his refusal to vary the bright white lighting, which remained unchanged throughout the evening. At the Old Vic the director was Michael Benthall, who seemed to me more talented (at least on this occasion) as a choreographer than at handling the action. Edith Evans was to play Queen Katharine. She arrived for rehearsals a few days late, as she was finishing her scenes in a film, *The Nun's Story,* in which she had been enraptured by working with the director Fred Zinnemann. She was in somewhat obstinate mood, determined to defy the denunciatory traditions of Mrs Siddons and Sybil Thorndike, and she played the death scene of Katharine with moving subtlety. But in the earlier scene when the Queen defies the Cardinals, she insisted on sitting in a chair. I ventured to suggest to her that this might anticipate her effect in the final scene, but she refused to consider changing it. The stage at the Vic is not very wide, and in the trial scene both Katharine and Wolsey were encumbered by enormously long trains, and we spent the whole scene moving past each other warily to avoid them getting entangled.

On the opening night we were all extremely nervous, and the royal pair (Edith Evans and Harry Andrews) both dried up disastrously in their first speeches, one after the other, sitting on their thrones under the blazing lights. When I, who was next to speak, managed to remember my lines correctly, I felt like a smug schoolboy showing off before the class. The pictures I had seen of Irving as Wolsey showed him haughty and ascetic, and I thought I might hope to make the same effect. But I did not succeed with my performance, even though after the first night I padded my costume and reddened my cheeks to look more the vulgar butcher's son.

Vivien Leigh criticised me severely for shedding real tears in the scene of Wolsey's downfall, and I learned to take heed of what she had said. I certainly weep on the stage far too easily, just as Ellen Terry said she did. In certain parts it is legitimate to shed tears in an emotional scene: in the later scenes of *Richard II* and in the statue scene at the end of *The Winter's Tale*, for example, I thought my weeping perfectly legitimate. Then, long afterwards, in David Storey's *Home*, I was supposed to cry at different times for several seconds. This I found quite easy to do. I pride myself, after long experience, that I can begin and stop weeping at the exact points demanded in the script.

When the opening of the National Theatre was finally announced, I implored Ralph Richardson to offer to revive his definitive Falstaff and suggested that I might play the old King Henry IV, and that two younger stars – Albert Finney and Paul Scofield – perhaps, might agree to play Hotspur and Prince Hal. But Richardson firmly refused my idea, which I have deeply regretted ever since.

However as the part of the King had always appealed to me and I had never acted it on the stage, I was delighted when Orson Welles proposed I should play it in his film *Chimes at Midnight*, although I had been somewhat overwhelmed by his massive personality on two separate occasions in former years.

On the first of these, Ralph Richardson and I had been recording together a long series of Sherlock Holmes episodes for radio in which he played Dr Watson and I was Holmes. Halfway through the recordings we heard that Welles was coming over, for a single day, to play the villainous Dr Moriarty. We took him out to lunch at the Étoile restaurant in Charlotte Street, and all the other customers turned their heads in amazement as Orson held forth with Churchillian emphasis, wielding a huge cigar in one hand and gesticulating vividly with the other. We felt like two schoolboys being taken out by a kind relative at half-term.

I next encountered him in Vivien Leigh's dressing-room at the St James' Theatre in King Street (where she was later to lead a violent demonstration to try and prevent it being pulled down), and found we were both to be weekend guests at Notley

Abbey in Buckinghamshire, the Olivier country home. In the car I ventured to ask Orson what he was doing in London. 'I'm going to play Othello,' he replied. To which I rashly responded, 'On the *stage*? In *London*?' – a remark which he greeted with a grunt of disapproval.

Next morning he left early for London, and we did not see him again till late on the Sunday evening, when he appeared ravenously demanding something to eat. The staff had already gone to bed, but Vivien Leigh, always the perfect hostess, went off to make him scrambled eggs. I enquired whether his trip to town had been successful. 'Not at all,' he answered, 'she cried the whole time.'

After such a typical example of my tactlessness I hardly expected to hear from him again; but, to my great surprise, he offered me an engagement to play his father in a film version of Kafka's *The Trial* which he was making in Paris. Various people counselled against accepting, saying that I should probably not be paid, and I turned down his offer (I think he finally played the part himself). But when some years later he wrote offering me the old King in *Chimes at Midnight*, I was greatly flattered and excited. It turned out to be a most amusing experience, though not without certain disadvantages.

No costume designs and fittings were arranged in London and I was told that everything would be finalised when I arrived in Spain. Orson himself was filming on location, and, when I was met at the airport by some of his assistants, they told me that the best hotel in Madrid refused to house any more actors owing to the bad behaviour of certain stars who had been to stay there some months before. So I was driven thirty miles out of the city to a dingy hotel near the Escorial, where I spent the night rather apprehensively. As soon as I woke next morning, some people arrived with an armful of extremely shabby costumes and chain mail, which I tried on hastily with some distaste. Then I was driven some miles to a large meadow, where Orson was directing the Battle of Shrewsbury, and I found myself being hastily made up and thrust bewilderingly into a scene with the minimum of rehearsal.

Orson welcomed me charmingly and seemed to take everything for granted. A few days later we travelled to Barcelona and were billeted in a small hotel in the mountains above the city, usually open only in the summer but specially reopened for our benefit. It was November: beautiful sunshine most of the day, but very chilly by the end of the afternoon. We lunched on an outdoor terrace, but most of the shooting was in a huge, romantic looking building (it had, I think, once been a prison) with all the windows smashed and stone floors. But it made a fine cathedral-like setting for the court scenes in which I was involved.

The organisation was somewhat chaotic, but I was lost in admiration for Orson's unfailing flair in choosing his set-ups for the camera, encouraging me – with extremely perceptive appreciation of the Shakespeare text – and managing several of the Spanish supporting cast who spoke no English. He trudged about tirelessly and was extremely considerate, sending out for brandy which we sipped huddled over a small electric fire. I badly needed the attention, since I was naked to the waist, with only a thin dressing gown and tights to protect me from the evening chill.

As usual with Welles, he was very short of money. I was to work for only about ten days altogether; Margaret Rutherford, Jeanne Moreau, and Alan Webb could each be paid only for a week, and their scenes were all shot after I had left. Keith Baxter, who played Prince Hal, was the only actor to work all through the weeks of filming. He had acted before with Orson, whom he admired tremendously, and the two became devoted friends.

There were twenty or thirty extras, also Spanish, who seemed to be wandering about demanding more money, and as there were no kind of sanitary facilities on the premises, the results were apt to be unsightly and demoralising, to say the least. Orson suffered from eczema and couldn't wash his hands, and was interrupted at intervals by worrying decisions about two other uncompleted films, *Treasure Island* and *Don Quixote*, on which he had already started working sporadically in other parts of Spain. But I grew to be tremendously fond of him, and was very sorry to come away. I never even saw him made-up as Falstaff, but on my last day of shooting he suddenly asked me to take part in a moment when I had to look at Falstaff (off-camera), then at the Prince, then at someone else. I had no idea how this would emerge in the final film, but when I finally saw it, it turned out to be a most effective close-up!

The following summer I happened to be in Paris. *Chimes* was being shown at one of the cinemas in the Grands Boulevards, and I hastened to go in to see it for the first time. As I took my seat, an actor was on the stage appealing for some charity or other.

As I came out into the street after it was over, I found to my dismay that my reading glasses and sunglasses had both vanished from the outside pocket of my jacket, which I had taken off in the cinema, as it was a very hot afternoon. Trying, in my extremely halting French, to explain my loss, first to the ticket office and then to one of the usherettes, I was greeted with delight by both of them, who recognised me from my close-ups on the screen. The poor actor was again making his charitable appeal to the audience, but his efforts were interrupted as all the lights in the cinema were suddenly turned on, and the occupants of the row I had been sitting in were asked to vacate their seats. My two pairs of glasses were hastily retrieved from the gap at the side of the seat I had occupied, and I retreated to the exit in great confusion, fearing that everyone would think I had staged the whole episode simply to draw attention to myself.

CHAPTER SIX

Scenery • Costumes

In my early boyhood I was enraptured by the great fairytale illustrators of the period: Arthur Rackham, Edmond Dulac, Kay Nielsen. As a schoolboy, I was to discover Aubrey Beardsley, and I was extremely fond of an edition of *A Midsummer Night's Dream* with most imaginative drawings by Heath Robinson, who was more usually noted for his comic pictures of machinery. In my enthusiasm, I even attempted to imitate some of these artists in many amateurish designs which I showed off conceitedly in the family circle. Falling passionately in love with the theatre from my teens, it was mostly the pictorial magic that I most appreciated. Box-set interiors left me cold, and the more changes of scene that were provided the happier I would be.

Avidly reading the books of Gordon Craig, and fascinated by the work of Claud Lovat Fraser – whose fourteenth-century missal designs for *As You Like It* and masterfully simple décor for *The Beggar's Opera* I had seen at the Lyric Hammersmith – I began to cherish a fruitless ambition to become a stage designer myself. I slaved away building miniature settings in the studio attic of my South Kensington home, trying to realise the steps and alleys which I remembered in such elaborate detail from my repeated visits to the Oriental splendours of *Chu Chin Chow*. When I finally decided to try to become an actor, I became rather more critical of scenery and costume, looking for the sort of pictorial detail that I found at the National Gallery and the Tate, which ranged so widely in style and periods.

Greatly as I admired the shadowy loftiness of James Pryde's scenery for Paul Robeson's *Othello* in 1930, I realised that the scenes were placed too far back on the stage, dwarfing the actors. In contrast the staging of *A Midsummer Night's Dream* by Norman Wilkinson in the Granville-Barker production (which I had been lucky enough to see in 1913) with its forest suggested by long green curtains, crowned with a white floral chandelier, provided an elegant background for his gilded fairies.

I still believe, that for young people going to the theatre for the first time, pictorial beauty brings an immediate response quite apart from the action of the play itself and the actors taking part in it. I cannot believe that Shakespeare's plays are more easily accepted by a youthful audience when transposed into another period, though I also think that the first experiments of staging the plays in modern dress did much to break with the spectacular Edwardian productions which so delighted our forebears. We all know, of course, that kings and queens only wear their crowns on ceremonial occasions and not in private life. But in Shakespeare's plays ceremonial occasions are very frequent, and nondescript figures in lounge suits addressing their subjects through microphones are hardly an effective or impressive substitute. Of course, nobody would wish for a return to the Royal Academy productions of palaces and castles, or the pictured gardens and forests contrived with branches stretched on netting and backcloths with painted vistas and landscapes, alternating with flapping front-cloths or flimsy curtains. I soon realised how important speed in scene-changes and economy of superfluous decoration was in mounting Shakespeare's plays to their best advantage, especially since our admirable reversion to very full texts.

When I first embarked on the hazardous adventure of trying to direct Shakespeare myself, I naturally attempted to realise a few of my own cherished ideas, and also found the greatest interest and delight in working with a number of expert designers – among them, Mariano Andreu, Motley, Leslie Hurry, Sophie Fedorovitch, James Bailey and, despite occasional tantrums, Oliver Messel and Cecil Beaton.

Peter Brook is, I think, the most brilliantly gifted of all the designers I have ever worked with. His incredible range of styles and versatility has never ceased to arouse my unstinted admiration, and his staging of *Measure for Measure, Titus Andronicus, King Lear,* Seneca's *Oedipus,* and the beauty and originality of his famous *Midsummer Night's Dream,* will always remain among my most treasured memories.

As I watched this year's production of *The Wind in the Willows* at the Olivier Theatre and marvelled at the scenic invention and its manipulation, I rejoiced at the enchanted reactions of the young audience. It was a welcome return to the magic of the live theatre, now so wonderfully enhanced, when used imaginatively, by the wonders of computerised cueing and by the subtleties of today's lighting equipment. Might it not now be possible to present one of the great Shakespeare plays with a similar combination of talent and invention without, I venture to hope, a neglect of pictorial beauty?

Bernard Shaw came to RADA when I was a student and talked about Shakespeare's use of the depth of the stage. He said it is important, for instance, in Mercutio's death scene in *Romeo and Juliet,* that there should be entrances from the back of the stage on either side, to give the impression of streets. He explained that at Oberammergau, one of the great moments of the Passion Play was when you saw Christ with the cross appearing at one door far up-stage, and at the other entrance, also far upstage on the other side, the Virgin Mary and the other women, and you knew that when they came down the stage they would meet. He said the same effect should apply when Benvolio tells

Romeo, 'Here comes the furious Tybalt back again.' In other words, the audience should anticipate an important climax before it actually happens.

When I worked with Peter Brook I saw how extremely clever he was at designing a V-shaped set. He was one of the few people who really conquered the difficulties of the stage at Stratford. In *Measure For Measure* he designed a triangular scene, with the point nearest the audience, so that the action was pushed downstage from both sides. In the Elizabethan period of course, there was not that shape of stage at all, and I cannot understand how the groundlings, who could hardly see the inner stage when it was far back, could have followed what was going on there. But I suppose the scenes that were played on the balcony above were fairly easy to follow. Of course, in the eighteenth century all the actors came right down to the front and played directly to the audience. There have always been arguments among the actors I have known about how much you should play to the front, especially in soliloquies.

Beerbohm Tree was famous for having real rabbits in the Forest of Arden, and his tableaux – Cleopatra with pyramids looming, and Richard II riding a horse through the streets of London – delighted his Edwardian public. Although there were a lot of brilliant critics, such as Max Beerbohm and Bernard Shaw, who deplored these pictorial intrusions, the average theatregoer of the time really went for the occasion, to be seen by and mingle with the people they knew, just as they did at the opera. There were splendid first nights at His Majesty's, and anniversaries and jubilees were tremendously well done. To his great credit, Tree put on a festival of Shakespeare every year, during which he used to invite other companies to appear as well as his own, and seven or eight Shakespeare plays would be staged over a couple of weeks. I suppose this was possible in those days because labour was so cheap.

When I asked how Irving managed to tour in repertory, with

three or four plays given in the same week, I was told that the scenery was kept on carts or down at the railway sidings in trucks, and after every performance it would be struck and taken down to the station, where it would be exchanged for other scenery which was brought back to the theatre for the next night's performance. It was an extraordinary thing to stage so many plays in so few days. How the plays were lit in so short a time I cannot imagine, but obviously the lighting was not as complicated as it is today. Irving lit with gas and never believed that electric light was equally good, but Tree used a great deal of electric light. He even had Oberon's costume fitted up with electric light and the part played by a lady, who sang some of her speeches with the help of Mendelssohn.

Tyrone Guthrie had a genius for filling and emptying the stage and in putting life into the smaller parts, though he had an Irish streak of freakishness which I thought was apt to make his brilliant work uneven. Brook is enormously selective and consequently more powerful in his results. His crowds and the actual placing of the characters on the stage are equally brilliant. He is a master of deployment on the stage, while Guthrie was always, despite his talent, something of a scoutmaster. He was also obsessed with the theory that the actors must be close to the audience, who should ideally be seated around them. I admit the open stage has its advantages. You can speak more intimately, and the audience, particularly the ones close to you, can see your expressions very much better. But at the same time it makes the actors very vulnerable. An open stage (at the Round House, for instance, and at Chichester) forces the actor to turn continually so that the different parts of the house can see their faces. I played only once at Chichester and was extremely unhappy with the result. And when I saw an extremely good production at the Round House of Webster's *The Duchess of Malfi* (which I knew pretty well because I had played in it at the Haymarket under Rylands during the War),

ne banqueting scene,
cbeth, Piccadilly, 1942.

Left: 'He came on as a black s
Laurence Olivier as Macbet
Stratford on Avon, 1955.

Below: 'Well if I can't see the
cocky, do you wonder the aud
can't either?' Ralph Richardso
Margaret Leighton in *Macb*
Sratford on Avon, 1952.

Angelo in *Measure for Measure,* Stratford on Avon, 1950

Peggy Ashcroft
Portia in *The
Merchant of Ven*
Old Vic,
1932.

Peggy Ashcroft as Portia,
Stratford on Avon, 1953.

'I tried to make him a squalid little guttersnipe.' Shylock, with Peggy Ashcroft as Portia, Queen's Theatre, 1938.

Benedick with Peggy Ashcroft as Beatrice, Stratford on Avon, 1950.

Angelo with Maxine Audley as Mariana, Stratford on Avon, 195(

'His eyes have the curious sightless blaze of a man obsessed with a ideal.' Cassius, with (*seated left to right*) Paul Hardwick as Messala : Harry Andrews as Brutus, *Julius Caesar*, Stratford on Avon, 1950.

'A Shakespeare record for the longest run of the play.' Leontes with Camillo (Michael Goodliffe) and Mamillius (Robert Anderson), 1951.

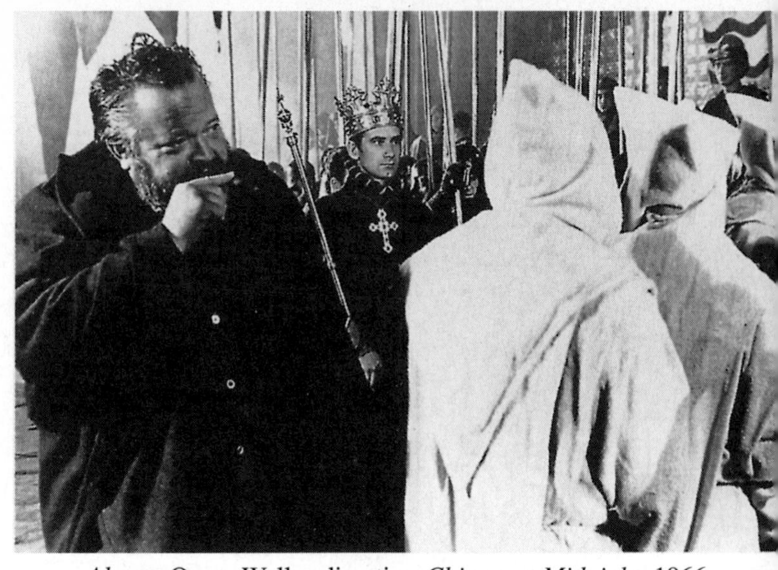

Above: Orson Welles directing *Chimes at Midnight,* 1966.

Below: King Henry IV at the Battle of Shrewsbury, with Keith Baxter as Prince Hal, *Chimes at Midnight*, 1966.

'A notable Othello, but he could show a dangerous adherence to stage tradition.' Godfrey Tearle as Othello, Stratford on Avon, 1948.

I reddened my :heeks to look nore the vulgar butcher's son.' /olsey in *Henry VIII*, Old Vic, 1958.

'An El Greco he
mit.' Prospero i
The Tempest,
Stratford on Avc
and Drury Lane
1957.

'A virile Renaissance
notable.' Prospero
with Jessica Tandy
as Miranda,
Old Vic, 1940.

Peter Brook emphasised the grand clothes and majesty at the end.'
Prospero, 1957.

'Peter Hall wanted me to look like Dr. Dee.' Prospero, National Theatre at the Old Vic, 1974.

Above: 'Prospero beginning to become inspired to write the play.' *Prospero's Books*, directed by Peter Greenaway, 1991.

Below: 'Magic effects of all kinds.' *Prospero's Books*.

With Mark Rylance as Ferdinand and Isabelle Pasco as Miranda in *Prospero's Books*.

Michael Clark as Caliban in *Prospero's Books*.

Above: 'Greenaway is influenced by all the great Renaissance painters.' The banquet scene in *Prospero's Books*.

Below: 'Out of the books he proceeds to create a new Kingdom.' The huge library set in *Prospero's Books*.

'I was greatly impressed by his control.' On the set of *Prospero's Books* with director Peter Greenaway.

I could hear only about half the dialogue, and this made it impossible to follow the very complicated Jacobean text. I never saw a production at Stratford Ontario, Guthrie's own theatre, which he designed and developed from a tent and which was said to work wonderfully. Both Irene Worth and Alec Guinness (who acted in the opening productions, *Richard III* and *All's Well*) were very happy and successful there. In all Guthrie's productions I was enormously struck by the way he arranged matters so that the stage would suddenly be empty or suddenly full; his groupings, entrances, and exits were most skilfully arranged. But I always thought he was inclined to shy away from the big emotional scenes in Shakespeare, frightened perhaps of the actors standing still and being dull. He tended to be embarrassed by love scenes, too, and would leave the actors to work them out for themselves.

Franco Zeffirelli can be depended on to create a wonderfully lively stage: the street scenes in his *Romeo and Juliet* were wonderful. But I did not care much for the lyrical scenes, and I have never thought that the lovers should actually be seen in bed together.

I do not like Shakespeare being acted in any period later than Jacobean, because it seems to me that if you are playing in Restoration costume with big wigs, in eighteenth-century costume with white wigs and high heels, or in Victorian clothes with full skirts, strapped trousers and frock coats, you cannot sit or stand or move except in the way these clothes demand. The furniture makes different demands too – the way you sit on chairs or sofas. If you are trying to speak Shakespeare's English it complicates matters to set the play in any period later than that of Charles I. Tyrone Guthrie did several Edwardian productions of *All's Well* and *Troilus and Cressida*, and I could not bear them. Not being familiar with either of these two plays, I could not follow the action at all easily.

My own production of *Much Ado* at Stratford in 1949 was set in the 'Piero de la Francesca' period, but several revivals that have been done since have been in Victorian dress, which seems to me outrageously wrong. How can you have a play which is entirely dependent on sexual innuendo and wit spoken by ladies and gentlemen dressed in a period when people covered up their piano legs because they were supposed to be improper?

John Bury designed for me a marvellous cloak in the Peter Hall production of *The Tempest* at the National Theatre in 1974, but it was so heavy that I could hardly lift it to put it round my shoulders. Clothes make a tremendous difference, especially in a big tragic part. When we did the Noguchi *Lear* in 1955 my costumes destroyed any chance of my giving an effective performance. He had designed only for ballet before. In *Lear* you have got to be dressed in comfortable, loose clothes. When I played *Othello* Zeffirelli designed for me impossibly heavy robes. The production was a dead failure, and for the second performance I sneaked up to the wardrobe and got out a lot of old kaftans that Anthony Quayle had worn three years before.

I think to dress a Shakespearean play in a 'non-period' is perhaps the best solution, as in the Trevor Nunn *Macbeth*. I would be prepared to see most of the plays done not too realistically as regards costume. But of course the look of the stage greatly affects the response of an audience. I have always had such a love of the pictorial side of the theatre that the first things in a production that really strike me are the scenery and dresses: if they delight me I am halfway to enjoying myself already.

I don't know whether I would have enjoyed the productions of Beerbohm Tree and Irving. Irving's were evidently mysterious and atmospheric, though I dare say I would not have found much of the acting very good. Tree obviously overdid things and had far too much scenery and spectacle, but as a young man I would have loved that. I very much enjoyed a lot of the rather spectacular scenery and dresses at Stratford in the Forties and Fifties designed by Leslie Hurry, Oliver Messel, James Bailey and others, and I cannot see that it is any disservice to Shakespeare to have the stage looking beautiful. But I don't like the plays to be staged too blatantly out of period. Guthrie, for instance, had Helen of Troy in *Troilus* playing the piano dressed as the Merry Widow.

CHAPTER SEVEN

Company Ensembles • Shakespeare the man • 'Effects'

All the study and criticism in the world cannot make the production of a Shakespeare play exciting unless the essential quality of the play is revealed on stage, rather than in the director's notes. Granville-Barker was like the conductor of an orchestra. He could bring out qualities in actors that they didn't know they had. Shakespeare stands up to strange treatment almost better than anybody, but I resent it all the more when people take liberties with the plays. I think it as insulting as it would be to hear a great orchestral score played sloppily and with the movements transposed. After all, in a great orchestra, every instrumentalist is an expert; whereas in no Shakespeare production I have ever seen have more than five or six of the actors been perfectly chosen and controlled.

I do not think all-star casts help either. The difficulty is to find a superb all-round company, with one or two striking personalities to lead it. It is something we have never had in England, though the Berliner Ensemble, the Stanislavski Theatre, and some of the other great foreign companies (such as the Comédie Française in its great days) seem to have achieved it; yet many foreigners, especially Americans, proclaim that England has the best actors in the world.

Irving's company was obviously perfectly adequate to support him and he worked furiously to train them. Beerbohm

Tree tried to outdo him in the way he staged the plays, but he also had much finer casts. He engaged many of the most promising actors of the day (Lyn Harding, Lewis Waller, Laurence Irving and many others) to act with him, which was surprisingly generous, because he was himself obviously a rather hit-or-miss character actor himself. Many famous stars had their first successes under him, and he clearly had a great gift for creating an exciting company.

I greatly admired Guthrie's first modern-dress *Hamlet*, with Alec Guinness, just before the war. At the climax of the play scene, at the exit of the King, everybody was rushing about the stage, and the boy who was playing the Player Queen was standing in someone's way and Rosencrantz knocked him down and sent him spinning into the wings. This moment was so beautifully timed and placed that the whole audience gasped, fearing he had been really hurt. But this suddenly took all the attention away from the play.

There was a lot of comic business in Guthrie's *Henry VIII* – godmothers sneezing in the middle of Princess Elizabeth's christening, bird-droppings falling onto people's heads when they were walking through the streets – yet he had skated over quite important scenes and had not rehearsed them thoroughly. Again, in the Guthrie *Hamlet*, it was obvious the director had spent little time or thought on the letter scene between the King, Queen and Polonius, but had some of his best inventions in other scenes – the umbrellas in the graveyard scene, for instance, and the Queen falling from a high rostrum to her death. In the play scene Ophelia was in full court dress with a white satin train and feathers in her hair, and Hamlet lay at her feet and put his hands up her clothes – very effective, but just a bit too sensational, as I think so many modern stunts in Shakespeare are.

The plays will always survive these experiments, of course. Something interesting will often emerge from them, and I suppose nearly every fantastical avant-garde production of Shakespeare has helped to open some doors, as Barry Jackson's first modern-dress Hamlet in plus-fours in the Twenties certainly did, though I greatly disliked it at the time.

When I played Shakespeare in Edward Bond's *Bingo* in 1974 I found the play had many fascinating qualities, but I could not get over the fact that the poet was drawn without any sense of humour. I had a feeling that the playwright had wanted to denigrate Shakespeare in his play, and when he found he could not succeed in doing so he gave him nothing to say at all. In the first act I spent the whole time sitting in silence looking out into the audience. Later on I had some beautiful, poetic and violent speeches, but all that the play seemed finally to suggest was that Shakespeare became a rather bitter businessman in his old age. The best scene was the one with Ben Jonson, in which the fine comedian Arthur Lowe was able to bring the play to life for the first time.

Many people have attempted to write plays about Shakespeare's life and work. As a young man I was very much taken with Clemence Dane's play *Will Shakespeare,* written in romantic blank verse, which Basil Dean directed. I was at the first night at the Old Shaftesbury Theatre, when Haidée Wright, who was a tiny little woman but a splendidly intense actress, played Queen Elizabeth marvellously well, besides having the best speeches in the play. Philip Merivale was Shakespeare, Claude Rains played Marlowe, and a splendid old actor called Arthur Whitby (who had been Toby Belch with Granville-Barker) appeared as Henslowe.

There were some ridiculous things in the play. In the first act the boy Shakespeare was planning to leave Ann Hathaway, but she was given all the sympathetic lines, and later appeared at intervals throughout the play (in a transparency) mourning her departed husband, so that poor Shakespeare was made to seem an utter cad. In the first act he fell asleep by the fire and characters from all the plays moved about in the shadows – Lady Macbeth, Ophelia and so on – in a kind of pageant. Finally in the last scene, in an interview with Queen Elizabeth, Shakespeare turned her out of her own throne room while he sat down to write a new play, which was not very likely or convincing. Clemence Dane was a gifted, many-sided writer, but her plays and novels were not destined to be long remembered.

I knew very few of the Sonnets until I came to speak some of them in my recital *Ages of Man*. Later I recorded many of them for Howard Sackler. I have never been able to understand them completely, but I always tried to take some comfort from Shaw's remarks about *Othello, The Tempest,* and *Antony and Cleopatra,* when he says that in many of the great speeches the sound often matters more than the sense. The text, he says, should sound like the swaying of forest trees, evoked by the range of the verse – in Othello's ' . . . like to the Pontic Sea,' for instance, in Cleopatra's mourning at the death of Antony, and in 'the cloudcapp'd towers' of Prospero.

As a child I saw few of the great Shakespearean actors, though I remember seeing Godfrey Tearle as Othello at the Royal Court in 1919 or 1920 and being enormously struck by his performance. When I came to meet him later on he gave me the impression that, like myself, he was neither a great thinker nor a great scholar. Henry Ainley had a marvellous voice and personality, but oddly enough was not very good in Shakespeare (although under Granville-Barker he was said to have been wonderful as Leontes and as Malvolio). Certainly when I saw him as Macbeth, with Sybil Thorndike, he was no good at all; and he was dreadfully bad as Prospero, when he did not seem to concentrate. But maybe he was too old by the time I saw him play.

I think many of the best actors are instinctive rather than intellectual. Sybil Thorndike was far more many-sided than Edith Evans, but Edith was the greater actress. Her Rosalind was a marvel, though she was nearly fifty when I saw her play the part. Sybil Thorndike knew about all sorts of things outside the theatre, but Edith Evans had not many other interests; for instance, I think she knew nothing of music. And she often spoke nonsense when she talked about her own acting. She could give you all sorts of wrong explanations for things she instinctively did superbly well. She was inimitable as the Nurse in *Romeo and Juliet* in 1935; her Rosalind was dazzling, and she was equally good when she played Emilia to Richardson's Iago in 1932. Her Helena in *The Dream* at Drury Lane had not been a success, and it was because she knew she had played Helena so badly that she went to the Old Vic in 1924, and some years afterwards advised me to do the same.

An actor does not need to be intellectual or scholarly (whether a director should be is another matter). I was wonderfully lucky to make a success in Shakespeare because I have a great tradition from my forebears, which stood me in very good stead and gave me a feeling for wearing costume and speaking verse. But I have never had an intellectual approach towards the plays, and audiences often credit you with far more intelligence than you really possess.

Some stage actors find film acting more difficult than the theatre because of the lack of continuity of style and performance. It is, I think, almost equally difficult, but in a different way. I am no longer afraid of filming as I once was. For many years I was dreadfully self-conscious before the camera, chiefly because I felt I was not good-looking enough and because my mannerisms became exaggerated on the screen. But gradually I became fascinated with the medium and learned how to relax. In the theatre I had been greatly influenced by Komisarjevsky, working in Chekhov. And by playing many different kinds of parts over the years, I was lucky enough to learn to make use of a good many varieties of technique. Edith Evans used to say, 'I never make effects.' Well, I have always made effects whenever possible, and I think she did too, though she would never admit it. But when one talks about acting being effective, I suppose that means that it has the right effect for the audience; though a performance cannot have the same effect on everyone in front, where everyone is undergoing different reactions and having different recollections of what they saw, some of which they may not even remember correctly afterwards. In the same way, actors, especially in a long-running production, can become stale and fall back on tricks they have used in other plays. I was shocked to find in my later years (particularly during the Second World War, when I had rather an elderly company) how many good actors tended to fall back on past successes – on things they had used before to get a round of applause or a big laugh.

Of course, too great an awareness of audiences can be a danger if an actor begins to worry about what they are thinking. When you have been on the stage for many years and people have seen you many times, you know that they will come into the theatre with a lot of preconceived ideas. When I acted in the theatre in my later years, I would often think: 'Some of the audience have never seen me before, and may expect a great deal. Or they may expect me to be as bad as some people say I am, and I must not let that affect me. I must play the part as best I can and not worry about the reaction of the audience or even of the critics. If I seem to be thought good by my fellow actors that is the best satisfaction I can hope for.'

CHAPTER EIGHT

The Tempest • On Stage and Film

Komisarjevsky told me long ago that I ought to play Prospero looking like Dante, without a beard, and I was clean-shaven when I first appeared in the part at the Vic, though I did not repeat the experiment in later revivals of the play.

In Peter Brook's production of *The Tempest*, I conceived Prospero as a sort of El Greco hermit with very short hair: I was naked to the waist and had bare legs. Peter Hall said he wanted me to look like Dr Dee, the Elizabethan alchemist, and persuaded me to wear a beard and spectacles and voluminous robes, so that I felt very swaddled and confined. In some ways this is right for Prospero, but I was anxious to show him as a man who had lived with nature for many years. Brook and Hall also had completely different ideas about the end of the play. Brook felt that Prospero in the last act goes back to his dukedom as a kind of God; Hall was convinced, because of the Epilogue and Prospero's attitude in the last act, that Shakespeare means him to be disillusioned, very reluctant to take his dukedom back, and finally returning to it in despair, knowing that everything is beyond redemption except for the young people, who are a kind of forlorn hope. I did not altogether agree with this reading, but I thought it was very interesting to see if I could be equally convincing playing the part in another way.

Glynne Wickham, a professor at Bristol, thought that Shakespeare wrote the play to flatter James I for his achievement in bringing the kingdoms of England and Scotland together, and that in the masque one of the characters, Iris, is meant to be Queen Elizabeth because of the Rainbow portrait, while Juno represents Anne of Denmark, James's Queen. Knowing Westminster Abbey very well since the time when I was a schoolboy there, I was aware that there are two monuments in Henry VII's Chapel. When James came to the throne and joined the kingdoms of England and Scotland, he had his mother's body disinterred and brought back by torchlight to London where she was buried in a chapel next to Henry VII's tomb; then, in a similar chapel on the other side, he put the tomb of Queen Elizabeth. Wickham thought that Ariel goes up to Heaven as a kind of John the Baptist, to prepare for Prospero's (King James's) deification. This would lend greater credence to the grand clothes and majesty at the end of the play, which Brook's production emphasised, whereas Peter Hall's idea of the disillusioned writer getting old and despairing was the other side of the coin. Both are fascinating interpretations, and I found it very hard to choose between them.

Caliban is a difficult part. Ralph Richardson gave a marvellous performance at the Old Vic in 1930 (the first time he and I worked together) and succeeded completely in combining the comic elements and the pathos of the character. I once saw an old actor called Louis Calvert play Caliban. He was dressed in a kind of animal skin and walked about on all fours like a pantomime bear: quite ridiculous. Sir Frank Benson used to hang from a tree with a fish in his mouth, and Beerbohm Tree had a tableau at the end of the play in which Caliban was left lonely and forlorn on the island, crouching on a cliff with the ship sailing away in the distance.

In all the times I acted Prospero, I never looked at Ariel. He was always behind me or above me, and I saw him only in my mind's eye. Though I had always set great store by this effect,

I found I could not, for various reasons, use it in Peter Greenaway's film *Prospero's Books*, and so I tried to forget it altogether. In this film I had to wear enormously heavy cloaks and headgear, but this was not the same hindrance as I had found it with the great cloak which John Bury had designed for me in 1974, which I had had to sling around my shoulders myself. In the film I had other people to hang the cloak around me before I tried to act the scene.

I had always had a great ambition to film *The Tempest*, but I could not find a director until I happened to meet Peter Greenaway. I had been fascinated by his films, especially *The Draughtsman's Contract*, which I saw two or three times. He was a completely new personality, as you could feel from the way in which his films were photographed and acted.

I have not found it easy to meet film directors. I once tried to approach Akiro Kurosawa, but he never answered. Giorgio Strehler, who runs theatres in Milan, where he directs plays as well as operas, kindly gave me a cassette of his striking theatre production of *The Tempest* which he had taped for television. I was very taken with it, and thought perhaps he might be interested in directing it as a film; but he does not speak English, and I think he prefers to work with his own actors. I talked to Alain Resnais about the play, and to a number of other film directors at the times I worked with them, but none of them seemed to care for the idea. I always felt I would prefer an English director, Peter Brook, perhaps. But he is I think better in the theatre than in films (though I think his *Lear* film is greatly underrated), and now he works only with his own company. I wrote to Ingmar Bergman and begged him to come and talk to me about it, but he, too, refused. He is, it seems, a very private man and works only with people he knows well, but I had loved his wonderful *Magic Flute* film and thought he might be the man to give *The Tempest* the quality it really needs.

Benjamin Britten, to whom I talked a lot about my ideas on

several occasions, said he would be glad to compose the music for such a film. He had a fine idea that all the early part should be done with a backing of real sound – flagstones and cries, crashing seas and so on, but that once Prospero gets to the island, everything should be done with music, no footsteps or any natural sound, and of course he would have done wonders with Ariel's songs and his own particular feeling for the sea.

There had been talk of doing *The Tempest* on the screen several times. At one point it was announced that Michael Powell was going to film it in Yugoslavia, with James Mason as Prospero and Mia Farrow as Ariel. I was of course relieved when that project fell through. Derek Jarman asked me to be in his film, but I didn't care for his ideas. The BBC asked me to do it in their television series, but they warned they had very little money to spend, and when I suggested it might be shot in the Inigo Jones Banqueting Hall in Whitehall, they would not hear of it. I also talked for a few days with the controversial Peter Sellars, a young American who has since directed opera at Glyndebourne as well as in his own country. He came over and spent two weekends with me discussing the possibility of making the film, but I became rather distrustful of him, though he obviously has a lot of talent. Somehow, I did not think we would get on together, though he had some very original ideas. The film was to be backed by an American producer whom I knew slightly and who suddenly offered to do it, but only if I would use Sellars as director. Of course, I was very excited, but suddenly the backer telephoned from America (he did not bother even to write to me) to say that the money was no longer available. So, finally I gave up the whole idea. All I had to show for it was a short digest of some ideas I had of how the play could be filmed.

Then, out of the blue, Peter Greenaway rang me up to ask if I would appear for three or four days in a television film of Dante's *Inferno*. He said he would simply photograph my face in close-up while I spoke a lot of blank verse translated by a friend of his. So I went to a little studio in Hammersmith and we did three or four days work on the *Inferno*. This came out in 1990 and made quite a critical stir. Then, while we were having lunch one day, I said, 'You know, the one thing I long to do is to make a film of *The Tempest*'. Three months later I received from him a detailed script, devised for the screen, and containing the first part of the play, up to the meeting of Ferdinand and Miranda. A few months later he had completed the whole shooting script and sent it to me. It made an enormously thick volume, with every kind of detailed description of how the film was to be shot. The scenario is, I think, extraordinarily original and daring. It consists entirely of Shakespeare's text: there is not a word in it that is not in the play. But then he suddenly said, 'Why don't you play all the parts?' I replied, 'You must be mad. What about Miranda and Ariel?' I didn't really understand what he was driving at.

I don't think Shakespeare's plays can possibly be put on the screen just as they are in the theatre. The most successful have been the most imaginative, like the Russian *Hamlet*. One of the best, I think, is the American *Julius Caesar* that I was in with Brando, and of course the splendid *Henry V* of Olivier. Greenaway said, 'We'll call it Prospero's Books' (a reference to the books given him by Gonzalo that Prospero takes with him when he is turned out of Milan by the usurper and set adrift in the little boat with the infant Miranda). Out of the books he proceeds to create a new kingdom, which he will rule (as Prospero himself had once done) as a sort of Haroun al-Raschid emperor. I thought it all sounded very exciting, but I couldn't understand his idea of my playing all the parts. However, I trusted him and agreed to do it. I went rather apprehensively to a recording studio and taped the whole play for him, reading all the characters in turn.

We filmed in Amsterdam in the spring of 1990 and the final

editing was being completed in Japan in 1991. It is a perfectly authentic version of the play, but completely fantasised and elaborated by Greenaway in his own particular way. I imagine, from what little I have seen of it so far, that what might emerge is a kind of mimed ballet of the action, with Shakespeare's words spoken over it. On the screen you see Prospero beginning to become inspired to write the play.

Greenaway was very modest in the way he talked to me about his script. I had given him the few pages of ideas that I had worked out years before when I had once thought of being able to shoot the film in Japan. One of the few things that I suggested (and Greenaway seemed to like it himself) was dealing with the great problem of the long opening dialogue between Prospero and Miranda, when he talks about their early life and how he was thrown out of Milan. I thought that if this could be done in flashback and one saw him being turned out by the Fifth Column, cast adrift in the boat with his baby child and arriving in the Island, the birth of Caliban, Ariel imprisoned in the tree, and all the other events which are described in that long opening scene, it would make them far more vivid and exciting. And sure enough, when the script arrived Greenaway had conceived something of the kind. I had once shown my little notes to Ralph Richardson, and he said 'Oh, you can't do this kind of thing, putting in all sorts of scenes Shakespeare never thought of.' As I write this, I have not yet seen the film, only an hour of clips, and there is an enormous amount of editing still to be done, with magic effects of all kinds. Until it is finished I have no means of judging how it has succeeded. But I am perfectly sure that it will be very beautiful to look at. Of course, Greenaway is a painter himself, influenced by Tintoretto and Titian and all the great Renaissance painters, and he organises and choreographs all his scenes with remarkable taste and feeling for depth and colour.

He was working with a crew, most of whom he had used in

his other films, and a superlative French lighting man, Sacha Vierny, whose work is most imaginative, mysterious, and striking. There are magnificent sets and costumes, mostly in the Renaissance style, designed by two Dutchmen, Ben Van Os and Jan Raelfs, who have created the Renaissance palace which Prospero has built in his imagination. It was fascinating to be given the opportunity of trying to play this great part, which I now know so very well, in a new way, after playing it four or five times in the theatre. With Greenaway I had the same feeling that I had with Peter Brook, with Granville-Barker, and with Lindsay Anderson and Peter Hall, the feeling that I could trust their judgment and criticism and put myself entirely into their hands. I had the same experience with Alain Resnais in 1976, when I did the film *Providence*, which I came to regard as the only screen performance I could be proud of. I found that Greenaway is a great admirer of Resnais, and has never met him because he regards his work so highly.

It was an extraordinary experience in Amsterdam. We shot the film in about seven or eight weeks, working in three huge film studios which had once been aircraft hangars. The sets were built in a framework of huge stone colonnades. You rather had the feeling you were inside a cathedral. Inside this framework there were some magnificent insets, among them a huge library with masses of books and desks, and a cornfield where Miranda meets Ferdinand for the first time. There were crowds of mythological figures, mermaids, sirens and animals, monsters of every kind. I met the other actors only a few times, and I never worked with Caliban at all although I did a scene in which I shouted at him when he was in the water.

Greenaway gave me no directions as to how he wanted me to play my part, but he did give me the most enormously heavy robes to wear. I had a kind of Doge's headdress, and huge cloaks – one red, one blue, and one black – woven and embroidered in Japan. I had to walk up and down huge corridors in them and it took four people just to put them around my shoulders; these were designed by Emi Wada, who won an Oscar for her costume designs for *Ran*, the Kurosawa version of *Lear*.

Caliban is played by that extraordinary dancer Michael Clark. I saw him only in two scenes – when he came out of a kind of hole in a grotto, dived into a pool and swam about, and when he was pursued by Stephano and Trinculo, who are played by two Dutch comedians. Ferdinand is played by a talented young actor, Mark Rylance, who has already played Hamlet successfully (though clad in pyjamas!); and the Miranda is a beautiful French actress, Isabelle Pasco.

I have already described how I played the part for Peter Brook and Peter Hall, the one ending on an optimistic note and the other on a disillusioned one. I felt it was rather a good thing I had not really anything to do in the film which was in any way similar to what I had done on the stage. For instance, the whole of the great 'cloud capp'd towers' speech had to be spoken while I was walking in a procession. We had another long scene in which Greenaway wanted me to walk with people standing beside me, and when I said I could not see it that way, he understood and changed it at once. We were in great sympathy over everything, and the few times I did suggest or alter something he immediately understood what I was driving at.

Above all, I was greatly impressed by his control. A very quiet man who never raises his voice, he walked about the studio all day long, never sat down, and seemed to work equally easily with the sound man who was British, the lighting man who was French, all the crew who were of mixed nationalities, including a lot of Dutchmen, and the whole cast, extras of every nationality, all very obedient, even when working overtime. They did not seem to mind taking all their clothes off to play the visionary and mythological characters. Unlike the atmosphere on most film sets, no one ever had to shout for quiet; there was no hammering or tantrums or bad behaviour. The whole thing was wonderfully organised, and I greatly hoped that the final result would be all that it seemed to promise while we were shooting it.

POSTSCRIPT

TRADITION IN today's theatre is denigrated and yet loved at the same time. Modern productions of Shakespeare are apt to be very revolutionary and are either enormously admired or severely criticised. I find it hard to know just where I stand now after my own experiences in Shakespeare so long ago. I inherited many of the traditions of the Edwardian theatre, and possibly have even created some myself over so many years. All the swift changes in my time have torn me in many directions, but I have tried to adapt myself, in my own clumsy way, to as many of them as possible, with a varying record of success and failure.

I am delighted to think I may have contributed a little to the popularity of Shakespeare because I happened to be a successful actor at just the right time in stage history. I suppose I felt then as I imagine Kenneth Branagh must feel today – frightened of being over-praised and over-exploited. And today, of course, there are all the temptations of television and movies to distract one from the live theatre. It was part of my good luck that the managements I worked for gave me so much freedom to choose plays, casts and designers. I had a say in every department of the theatre, which I think is essential if you are to lead a company successfully.

Television and radio have, of course, helped to make Shakespeare more popular than ever before. Immensely larger audiences are now familiar with the plays because they have heard them over the radio and seen them on television. Even the most unlettered people nowadays know Shakespeare's most famous speeches. I realised in the Twenties the advantages there were of forgetting class differences by playing to a mostly working-class audience, free of the snobbery of the West End. I must confess I always hated touring, and I greatly admire the determination to pursue it shown by the late Anthony Quayle, McKellen, Pennington and others of the present generation; but I also toured a great deal in the years before the Second World War and learned much from playing to so many different types of audiences.

When I was in India in 1945, a Shakespeare enthusiast, who had visited London many years before, politely enquired of me: 'And how is Sybil Thorndike? She must be quite senior now.' As a belated senior myself I am well aware that my views of Shakespeare's plays and the productions of them are of little consequence and sadly out of date, though it has given me some pleasure to recall my early struggles and hazards in the many different circumstances which were of such importance to me throughout my long career.

I had never expected to have such fine opportunities away from the theatre, both in the cinema and television. It is curious that my first screen success should have been as Cassius, and that lately I should have been lucky enough to have the opportunity of fulfilling my life-long ambition to play the part of Prospero for the screen. I was as absorbed throughout my years as a director as I was as an actor, though when I combined the two occupations, as I did many times, I sometimes became too divided to maintain the necessary concentration required. When I was directed by others I learned a great deal from them. I did not make many enemies, though I was fairly autocratic in the theatre. I never had to be concerned with money matters, worked for sympathetic managers, was given a free hand in casting and choice of colleagues and designers, and very seldom had to work in plays I did not like. I always found rehearsals fascinatingly lively, matinee days extremely arduous, and long runs as difficult to sustain as they were valuable for practice and selectivity.

Often I failed to intimidate and was apt to listen to too many people, to appear unduly impulsive towards my colleagues and to change my mind too often. I have always been too fond of popularity and wanted everyone to like me. I have often been too timid and cowardly in my behaviour, dreading crises and quarrels because I was always so happy in the theatre. I should perhaps have been a better mixer and also a more formidable character. Olivier was not always an easy man. Like Irving he was feared as well as deeply respected, but both men inspired enormous devotion and enthusiasm in their companies, and I have always hoped to do the same.

'And thus the whirligig of time brings in his revenges.'

APPENDIX I

The Critics

As a youthful playgoer I came to know many of the leading theatre critics by sight. My parents would point them out to me on first nights – the eminent A.B. Walkley of *The Times*, shortly afterwards to retire, giving place to his aesthetic-looking successor, Charles Morgan, with his long hair and black silk opera-cloak; James Agate, portly and flamboyant with his spectacles pushed upwards on to his forehead, and the gloomy-looking Hannen Swaffer – black hair, black satin stock, and black coat sprinkled generously with cigarette ash, like a funeral mute from Dickens. Soon after I first began to play leading parts in London, I made the acquaintance of Alan Dent, a clever young Scotsman who was dramatic critic for the *News Chronicle*, and he introduced me to James Agate, for whom he also worked as secretary and occasional stand-in. I was, of course, impressed to meet such a well-known figure in the theatrical world, and delighted that he evidently thought my acting showed promise. But he was also apt to become rather possessive, demanding to know my future plans and advising me to consult him about them. I resented some of his sweeping prejudices, as when he peremptorily dismissed two of my favourite actresses, Peggy Ashcroft and Elizabeth Bergner, as being too 'mousy-pousy'.

Agate was a great snob, boasting of his knowledge of the French theatre and his personal friendship with Bernhardt. (His sister May, who was an actress, had studied with her in Paris, and she had often been an honoured guest in their mother's house.) He loved to be on greeting terms with most of the big stars of the period, such as Marie Tempest and Sir John Martin-Harvey, wafting his way between the tables at the Ivy at lunch-time or at the Savoy

Grill after a first night. He ventured to invite Princess Marie-Louise to dine at his flat, and was enchanted to find that they both shared the same hired waiter.

Much as I enjoyed many of his sprightly notices and the series of Ego books which were published over several years, I became increasingly aware of his frequently unprofessional conduct. On one occasion he made headlines when at the opening performance of Thornton Wilder's *The Skin of our Teeth*, with Vivien Leigh in the leading part, he swaggered down the aisle as he returned from the bar after the curtain had already risen for the succeeding act. Laurence Olivier, who had directed the play, rewarded him with a stinging slap as he returned to his seat. And when I appeared as Richard II – an important first night for me at the Queen's Theatre in 1937 – he failed to go back after the second interval and remained chatting to some of his cronies in the foyer. Marie Tempest, who was in the audience, noticed his behaviour. She called him over to her table at the Ivy the following day and gave him a severe dressing-down, which resulted in his returning to watch the last act of my production at the next performance and then writing an extremely favourable notice. But this episode was a warning to me to try to avoid meeting or knowing critics personally outside the theatre. In my early days it was seldom that the dramatic critics signed their reviews, and I do not remember being interviewed by any of them, as is now so often customary. It was not till some years after the War that the *Sunday Times* asked me to take part in a series of personal interviews with Harold Hobson, who was then their dramatic critic. Despite my previous apprehensions this turned out to be a tactful and enjoyable experience. But when I arrived in New York in 1936 to play Hamlet there, I was surprised and dismayed to find I should be expected to submit, for several successive days, to individual interviews with four or five of the principal dramatic critics, none of whom, of course, had ever seen me on the stage. Of course, I felt sure they would take an immediate dislike to my personality and opinions. It was a very daunting demand, though I did appear to survive it without unduly unsatisfactory results.

I have always thought what drudgery and discipline must be needed for a dramatic critic, perhaps not so very unlike some of the similar hazards which beset the actor. If the mannerisms and personality of a player affect a critic disagreeably, he is bound to find it difficult to keep a fair and perceptive attitude towards his work. And it must be a sore temptation, when a play has unalterably bored him, to parade his own literary skill and humour at the expense of the wretched performers who have failed to satisfy him.

Kenneth Tynan, like Agate before him, could write brilliantly of plays and acting he admired, but could also be cruel and destructive if he was bored. Bernard Shaw and Max Beerbohm, on the other hand, in their long years as dramatic critics, contrived to ridicule bad work with wit and grace, even when forced to sit through what must have been something of a torture for them. And the urgent necessity for most critics of an immediate reaction in order to meet a deadline must be an added responsibility. The critic must be ready to respond immediately, and trust to experience and perceptiveness, together with complete concentration, to shape his comments and conclusions clearly in the limited space allowed him. I confess I have always devoured my notices and never forget the unfavourable ones. The Lunts always used to say that they never read their reviews till at least six weeks after the first night. I have sometimes wished that I had the courage to do the same. But, on the whole, the press has been amazingly kind to me over so many years, and it is very pleasant to read some of the most flattering ones again (as well as others less enthusiastic) now that John Miller has diligently resurrected them for this book.

MACBETH

This year one goes to the Old Vic, and sees new plays. I do not mean merely that Mr Shaw has been canonised, the programme now featuring Little Plays of St Bernard. I refer to an even larger matter than the recent arrival of Androcles with the Dark Lady on his arm, namely, that Mr Harcourt Williams has so quickened the work and freshened the touch that all air of stale routine falls from the Shakespearean revivals. When I looked upon Puck, Bottom, and their rout at Christmas I wondered whether I had ever met these people before. They were new acquaintance. So with Macbeth. After some experience of horn-helmeted, cross-gartered, but otherwise unformidable thanes, the critic may naturally expect to find in the great verse something of the shard-borne beetle's drowsy hum, and to agree that the affair is usually as august as a church service of solemn state. Mr Harcourt Williams's production does not fob you off in that somnolent way. It takes you by the ears and eyes and by the very throat, and makes your fell of hair 'rouse and stir as life were in't,' as Macbeth said of his own horripilations. Swiftly you realise that *Othello* is not, after all, the most exciting play ever written. *Macbeth,* despite those bores the witches – is that a heresy beyond pardon? – has pride of place in hurricane attack.

Mr Williams could not have done this without two admirable leaders and a company that has greatly improved. It is not my habit to knock the meaning out of the high words of praise by throwing them, confetti-wise, over a myriad merely competent performances. When I say that Mr John Gielgud's Macbeth is magnificent I mean that it will last long in my mind whence a dozen other Macbeths have slipped. Mr Gielgud's acting has 'filled out,' as they say of growing boys. It has ripened into a rich masculinity. His delivery of verse is clear, strong, and various; in the vocal flow and rhetoric of acting he is the Henry Ainley of the rising generation. His Macbeth is finely virile, a hawk-like chieftain that first hesitates to pounce and then turns haggardly from bloody deed to bloodier. No subtle neurotic is here from the Italianate school of Macbeths, but a soldier turned criminal by a weak head and a strong wife. Mr Gielgud's performance is finely clear, every stage in the man's decline to the crown and his last rise to the loss of it is marked with the furrows of desperation and distress. The make-up, as well as the acting, is a fine kaleidoscope of ruin.

The same sense of time marks the straightforward strength of Miss Martita Hunt as Lady Macbeth. At first, reading the letter, she is plain housewife with an appetite for self-advantage; then, the wave of chance oncoming, she surges to its crest: in the last scene of all, the sleep-walking, she might well answer the question 'Whither?' with Hamlet's 'Into my grave.' The thing is complete from vigorous, aspiring womanhood to the pale corruption of a poisoned mind within a failing, fainting frame.

In this production every picture tells the story; there is no fussy obeisance to a historic masterpiece, but a first-rate piece of narrative stage-craft which keeps you alert, nervous, terrified, and at last, sated as if you were seeing the play for the first time. Mr Wolfit's Macduff and Mr Neil Porter's Banquo are excellent, and Mr Francis James, with a very interesting and intelligent performance, steers the part of Malcolm out of that dullness to which it often falls. But why oh why, must King Duncan forever be presented in the living image of Father Christmas? The likelihood is that he was a hard-fighting fellow of fifty and not a portly dotard swaddled in a beard of cotton wool.

IVOR BROWN,
Observer,
March 1930

HAMLET

By William Shakespeare

Is it a cold tribute to an actor to say that his Hamlet in the theatre gives pleasure of the same quality and measure as a private reading of the play? It should not be, for in a man's library is given his ideal performance, free of physical impediment; and Mr Gielgud's playing is, for one spectator at least, this performance's precise equivalent. To others it may well seem too little spectacular, too curbed in its emotional display; but indeed, Hamlet is not a flaunting part, though it is often so treated; it is not designed to provoke hot tears and shouting but to penetrate the soul by way of the intellect; and the first merit of Mr Gielgud's interpretation is that it does not throw up passionate mists with which to conceal confusions. From the chill, ironical menace of its opening to the fierce attack of the play-scene and the terrible rage at the burying of Ophelia it pursues its argument with a brilliant lucidity. Nothing is smudged or doubtful; everything is as decisive as the line in the pencil-drawing of a master.

The consequence is that the problems of Hamlet's indecision resolve themselves. What held him from action was not fear, not some obscure disease of the will, but a quick intellectual apprehension of the event. Deep in his mind was knowledge of action's futility. To say that he would have acted if he had been bolder or stronger or more naturally human is to miss the point; he would have acted if he had been less intelligent. This is the seed from which the varied beauty of Mr Gielgud's performance springs, and this is why it is completely satisfying to the mind – so satisfying in its application to the instance of Hamlet that imagination springs, as it does in a reading of the play, from the melancholy particular to the tragic universal. In this sense, the performance is deeply moving. It has the influence of a sky from which storm after storm has passed away, leaving a final and absolute serenity.

That one actor's performance should have this effect is made possible by the cast that surrounds him. Of these only one is at fault, and, indeed, the fault is not in her acting. Miss Jessica Tandy's appearance and temperament, the almost aggressive sprightliness of her, run contrary to Ophelia; but Mr George Howe's Polonius, not a buffoon but an unconscious wit, Mr Vosper's dark portrait of the King, Miss Laura Cowie's Queen – a little stupid as Hamlet's mother was – Mr Hawkins's Horatio, and Mr Devlin's Ghost are very distinguished company. Motley's setting is, in most scenes, beautiful if examined, and has the supreme virtue of submitting itself to the play.

The Times,
15 November 1934

TWO GENTLEMEN IN VERONA

Mr Olivier and Mr Gielgud

Romeo and Juliet
Revival of Shakespeare's Tragedy

Thursday evening was all that an evening in the theatre should be – exciting, moving provocative. Here in conjunction were the flower of Shakespeare's young genius and the best of young English acting talent. The producer was our leading Shakespearean actor, and the scenery and costumes were by the artists who had attained fame through the productions of *Richard of Bordeaux* and *Hamlet*. In other words Mr Gielgud had once more invested him in his Motley and given these young ladies leave to speak his mind.

Let me begin with a word or two about the production, normally tucked away at the end. The difficulty of producing plays written for the Elizabethan and transferred to the picture stage must always be resolved by compromise, which means that good and bad must go hand in hand. The good point about this production is that it enabled that fiery-footed steed which is this tragedy to gallop sufficiently apace.

Now, though the acquisition of speed has been a triumph, it has entailed certain sacrifices. For Mr Gielgud's, and consequently Motley's, method is a combination of the Elizabethan and modern stages, with Juliet's bedroom and balcony a permanent part of the setting. That people might walk beneath it the thing was supported on posts, so that it looked rather like a hotel-lift which has got stuck halfway up to the mezzanine floor. The device also precluded the full use of the stage, so that the action seemed to take place not so much in Verona as in a corner of it. I fault the lighting, too, in that gone were the sun and warmth of Italy and the whole thing appeared to happen at night, the tomb scene being the cheerfullest of all! The costumes were charming, even if the football jerseys of the rival factions reminded us less of Montague and Capulet than of Wanderers and Wolves. Elsewhere Motley have rightly differed from Dickens's Flora, who could not conceive any connection between Mantua and mantua-making. In the theatre there is every connection, and Motley have caught the spirit of the place and time, brilliantly for example in Romeo's case, though in Juliet's oddly reminiscent of the pre-Raphaelite way of looking at Ellen Terry.

Mr Olivier's Romeo

The ball, whose masks were those of hoopoes, puffins, and other outrageously-billed birds, brought up a very nice point. It had been more than whispered that presently Mr Gielgud, who plays Mercutio, and Mr Olivier, who plays Romeo, are to change rôles. At first sight this suggested a line much in vogue: 'Just think what Toucan do!' But Thursday night's experience persuaded one to the contrary. Am I in the foyer going to chip bits off my invention for the benefit of other critics? Why should Mr Gielgud pilfer his bright heaven for the benefit of another's Romeo? This means that Mr Gielgud had produced all of *Romeo and Juliet* except half the title part! If not he was more than human, though in any case it was probably not humanly possible at one fell swoop to denude Mr Olivier of his modernity and turn today's clipped speech into a passionate feeling for verse. Mr Olivier's Romeo suffered enormously from the fact that the spoken poetry of the part eluded him. In his delivery he brought off a twofold inexpertness which approached virtuosity – that of gabbling all the words in a line and uttering each line as a staccato whole cut off from its fellows.

In his early scenes Romeo appeared to have no apprehension of, let alone joy in, the words he was speaking, though this may have been due to first-night nervousness, since he improved greatly later on. But throughout one wanted over and over again to stop the performance and tell the actor that he couldn't, just couldn't, rush this or that passage. If ecstasy is present in this play it must be at the meeting in the Friar's cell, where Romeo's words hang on the air like grace-notes:

> Ah, Juliet, if the measure of thy joy
> Be heap'd like mine, and that thy skill be more
> To blazon it, then sweeten with thy breath

This neighbour air, and let rich music's tongue
Unfold the imagined happiness that both
Receive in either by this dear encounter.

This is music and must be spoken as music. Again, what is the use of Shakespeare writing such an image as: 'The white wonder of dear Juliet's hand' if Romeo is not himself blasted with the beauty of it? Never mind Shakespeare's precepts; his verse must be recited line upon line, here a little hurry and there a little dwell.

Apart from the speaking there was poetry and to spare. This Romeo looked every inch a lover, and a lover fey and foredoomed. The actor's facial expression was varied and mobile, his bearing noble, his play of arm imaginative, and his smaller gestures were infinitely touching. Note, for example, how lovingly he fingered first the props of Juliet's balcony and at the last her bier. For once in a way the tide of this young man's passion was presented at the flood, and his grief was agonisingly done. 'Is it e'en so? Then I defy you, stars!' is a line which has defied many actors. Mr Olivier's way with this was to say it tonelessly, and it is a very moving way. Taking the performance by and large, I have no hesitation in saying that this is the most moving Romeo I have seen. It also explains that something displeasing which I have hitherto found in Mr Olivier's acting – the discrepancy between the romantic manner and such ridiculous things as cuff-links and moustaches. Now that these trivia have been shorn away and the natural player stands forth, lo and behold he is very good!

Mr Gielgud's Mercutio

Mercutio is always a problem, for the reason that the Queen Mab speech, obviously inserted to satisfy an actor's demand, is not in keeping with that arch-materialist. In my opinion the way to play the part is to go all out for the sensualist, treat the speech as cadenza and in the way a fiddler will plonk one of his own into the middle of somebody else's concerto, bow, decline an encore, and then get back into the character! Mr Gielgud reverses the process and builds his Mercutio out of the Queen Mab speech which, of course, he delivers exquisitely. This means a new death scene and saying 'A plague o' both your houses!' with a smile which is all a benison. Not good Shakespeare, perhaps, but very beautiful Gielgud. In these circumstances Mercutio is not our old friend but a Frenchified version, say Théodore de Banville's:

> Jeune homme sans mélancolie,
> Blond comme un soleil d'Italie,
> Garde bien ta belle folie!

I agree that the last line chimes with Shakespeare since both Mercutio and Adolphe Gaïffe keep their lovely riot in the sense that in the drama and the poem neither lives long enough to lose it.

Miss Peggy Ashcroft's Juliet has been greatly praised. Certainly the eager and touching childishness of the early part could not be bettered, so that we prepared to be greatly moved. Personally, I found the performance heartrending until it came to the part where the heart should be rent. And then nothing happened, though all the appurtenances of grief, the burying of the head in the Nurse's bosom and so forth were present. When Juliet lifted her head, her face was seen to be duly ravaged, but she continued to the end with the same quality of ravagement, which as a piece of acting spells monotony. In my view Miss Ashcroft implied Juliet without playing her. That is to say she did not move me nearly so much as any of the children who have played in 'Mädchen in Uniform.' But then it is very difficult indeed, perhaps impossible, for any Mädchen to put on Shakespeare's uniform. Mr Granville-Barker dismisses as 'parroted nonsense' the saying that no actress can play Juliet till she is too old to look her. Let this acute observer produce an actress past or present to support him! According to a great critic of the eighties, Ellen Terry herself failed not only to conjure up the horrors of the charnel house but to make the scene impressive. Im my judgment Miss Ashcroft succeeded in the first half, only to fade away later. On the other hand the success so far as it went was complete.

Miss Evans's Nurse

I have not space to enumerate the admirable supporting cast, and can only congratulate Mr Gielgud upon a production triumphant everywhere despite the fact that Romeo cannot speak his part, Juliet cannot act more than half of hers, and Mercutio is topsy-turvy. To crown all, remains the Nurse, knocking the balance of the play into a cocked hat, just as would happen if the Porter were the centre of *Macbeth*. Miss Evans rules the entire roost. Obviously of the German-Flemish school, this is Agatha Payne metamorphosed into good instead of bad angel. It is a grand performance, and her pathos should teach young playgoers what pathos was in my young days. One felt that whenever such grief is heard in the theatre, Mrs Stirling's heart will hear it and beat, though it has lain for a century dead.

JAMES AGATE,
Sunday Times,
20 October 1935

JOHN GIELGUD AS ROMEO

LAURENCE OLIVIER TAKES MERCUTIO

Romeo and Juliet, at the New Theatre, is one of those productions whose memory the true theatre-lover will carry with him to the grave. Visiting it again last night, I was swept once more by the same almost intolerable sense of enchantment which I had experienced when the run of the play began.

Now that John Gielgud and Laurence Olivier have changed parts, the production, which could hardly gain much in emotional effect, gains greatly in artistic balance. Mr Gielgud's Romeo is more romantic than was Mr Olivier's, has a much greater sense of the beauty of language, and substitutes a thoughtfulness that suits the part for an impetuosity that did not.

And if there were doubts whether Mr Olivier was well cast as Romeo, there can be none about his Mercutio. This is a brilliant piece of work – full of zest, humour and virility. The 'Queen Mab' speech – that most famous of purple patches – went for rather less than usual; but it could be counted well lost, seeing that it gave us a perfect interpretation of one of the most effective small parts in all drama.

Peggy Ashcroft's enchanting Juliet and Edith Evans's magnificent playing as the Nurse have already been praised so highly by me that I can now find nothing more to say about either. George Howe, Frederick Lloyd, George Devine, and half-a-dozen others in the long cast do work of distinction.

W.A. DARLINGTON,
Daily Telegraph,
29 November 1935

ROMEO AND JULIET

In many details of this rendering Mr Gielgud has bettered his own instruction; and in speed, decision, and radiance it has gained considerably since the first night. The altering of the chief roles is also an advantage, for Mr Olivier brings to Mercutio a touch of the saturnine soldier as well as of the brilliant dealer in railery; he is termagant, but affectionately so, and the picture fascinates in a manner quite different from Mr Gielgud's smoother lineation of the raffish, sparkling chatterbox. That the Queen Mab speech may have been better spoken by Mr Gielgud is no criticism of Mr Olivier's performance, for that speech is only tied to the character by the flimsiest of connections. It may be heresy to suggest that Romeo is a great name, but not a great part. Yet I do suggest it. After Mr Gielgud's Hamlet it seems almost small. I have often wondered whether some mighty passage of grief has not tumbled out of the text; is it credible that such a gorgeous and confirmed spouter can have taken the news of Juliet's death so calmly and so silently? Again, the presence of the boy-actor always made Shakespeare go gingerly on the action side of love scenes, and this great tragedy of love is therefore not so much the show of love as the spouting of it. A glorious verbal fountain it is indeed, and Mr Gielgud tosses the words with a lucidity which does not break fluency, and with a loveliness of intonation which Mr Olivier lacked. It is a beautiful performance, less forceful in some ways, better formed in others, than Mr Olivier's. Miss Ashcroft has improved her Juliet in strength and clarity for the most part, but there is still need for putting check and pattern upon her grief in 'O serpent heart.' In the lighter aspects of the role she is consistently admirable. If it be argued that Miss Edith Evans's Nurse is too good by a quarter, so distracting one's attention from whole to part, there is no answer save that we don't mind. *Romeo and Juliet* is not supreme as an organic whole (the plot is too silly), but as an assemblage of incomparable noises, persons, lyrics, and metaphors. And what a personage Miss Evans makes!

Observer,
1 December 1935

QUEEN'S THEATRE

Richard II

By William Shakespeare

If this production were defective, criticism might yet be tempted to soften its defects and over-praise it, for the season that it begins – a season of great plays, each put on for limited and guaranteed runs – is one upon the success of which much good in the theatre depends. Its failure would give disastrous opportunity to those who cry that the living theatre is a sick man that cannot save himself. Fortunately it is too good to fail. There is no danger of over-praising it.

The key to Mr Gielgud's interpretation of the part is in Richard's speech when, after his abdication, he has considered his mirrored face and thrown the glass to the ground:

> 'Tis very true, my grief lies all within;
> And these external manners of laments
> Are merely shadows to the unseen grief
> That swells with silence in the tortured soul.

All his playing is a movement towards this climax, and, after the fall, a spiritual search beyond it. Some have objected to Mr Gielgud's more recent acting that he has become increasingly inclined to emphasize his mannerisms. It is, therefore, of the first importance to say clearly that this performance of Richard is not only more mature, but simpler in construction, than his performance of the same part years ago at the Old Vic. In certain passages, before the rebellion has brought misfortune on the king, a wish to indicate his frailty of character and, perhaps, his personal charm, leads Mr Gielgud into a smiling that is too frequent, and gives an impression of contrivance; but even these scenes are not mannered; they are played with a rare directness and integrity, so that the growth of the man in his despair of this world is felt to be a real growth, and the petulance of the beginning and the splendid agony of the end are linked each to each by early hints of a splendour within and by late reminders of a weakness not, even in prison, wholly transcended.

Of Miss Ashcroft it is enough to say that in this play she accepts a small part and plays it with admirable grace. The whole production is distinguished by the excellence of its proportion. The opening is made lively by the Mowbray, at once violent and secretive, of Mr Glen Byam Shaw; by the fierce Surrey of Mr Quayle; by Miss Dorothy Green's keen note on the Duchess of Gloucester and by Mr Michael Redgrave's introduction to a study of Bolingbroke so steady and lucid that, when at last he is silent on this throne, the silence is illumined by knowledge of him – his ruthlessness, his uncertain desire to be honest, his conflicting conscience. There is a rich, heavy Northumberland by Mr Frederick Lloyd; a sketch of York by Mr George Howe lighted by a perceptive wit; and studies of Gaunt and Carlisle by Mr Quartermaine and Mr Harcourt Williams that are fresh within the tradition. In sum, a beautiful, carefully studied and extraordinarily complete performance of the play – as alive and well-balanced as any we may reasonably hope for in our time.

The Times,
7 September 1937

KING LEAR

To be at the Old Vic last night, waiting in the somewhat dingy but much-liked auditorium for the curtain to rise, was to enjoy a sense of the first genuine theatrical occasion of the war. Occasions of the kind declare themselves not in the sheen of fresh paint, diamonds, and gardenias, but in the unmistakable stir of a common intellectual expectancy. This stir last night was sufficiently accounted for – if not by the names on the programme, real and imaginary, standing in what looked to be singularly apt juxtaposition, then by the whisper that Mr Harley Granville-Barker, making one of his rare descents from inspired theory to practice, had taken a hand in this production. Still, some theatrical occasions, however genuine in their beginnings, fade into insignificance before the evening has ended. This one did not.

The common expectancy was to become a growing and virtually silent excitement, as it appeared that Mr John Gielgud, given complete freedom by a production of large mould and controlled momentum to act Lear, was acting with a nervous force which, though it seemed at times to fall something short in physical toughness, yet enabled him to trace with a brilliant exactness Lear's progress from worldly to spiritual authority. The Olympian grandeur, the frets, the rages, the madness lit with flashes of savage irony and broken in upon by spiritual illumination – all these phases of the part he succeeded in treating as though they were a spontaneous product of the mind, but the simplicities at the end he surrounded with a stillness of beauty which is rarely achieved on the stage.

The particular strength of the performance rests upon the boldness – the bold recognition from the first that in this tragedy we are borne through realms of fantasy in which cold reason cannot find satisfaction. Mr Gielgud concerns himself little with the corporal infirmities of the old King. Such detail he sketches in lightly and adequately, but they are not suffered to become a load fettering him to the realistic plane. He trusts the verse and his power to speak it, as a solitary silver figure in the dark loneliness, he speaks the storm, and his trust is never at any vital point betrayed.

The producer, Mr Lewis Casson, likewise trusts to the play's stagecraft as Mr Granville-Barker has elucidated it and to a company whose accomplishment collectively and individually is equal to every demand made upon it. Miss Fay Compton's softly malevolent Regan, whose languorous grace is not disturbed by a mortally wounded husband's plea for assistance, Miss Cathleen Nesbitt's darkly envenomed Goneril, Mr Nicholas Hannen's shrewd detection of what is heroic and what is absurd in Gloucester, Mr Andrew Cruickshank's sinister courtesy winding itself into an outburst of sadistic fury, Mr Jack Hawkins's amused and extremely effective playing of the Bastard, Mr Robert Harris's illuminating study of Poor Tom, and Mr Stephen Haggard's skilful exercise in Elizabethanism as the Fool – these are a rare catalogue of reasons why it is possible to enjoy tragedy.

The Times,
16 April 1940

A GREAT HAMLET

Hamlet • Haymarket

Hamlet is not a young man's part. Consider how ill it becomes a stripling to hold forth on the life after death, the propriety of suicide, the nature of man, the exuberance or restraint of matrons, the actor's art, the Creator's 'large discourse.' But Mr Gielgud could not be of a better age; he is at the height of his powers; the conjunction is marvellously happy. When, fourteen years ago at the Old Vic, the curtain went up on the new Hamlet there was perhaps not very much there except infinite grace. Four years later, after the production at the New Theatre, I find that I wrote: 'The impression gathered is that of a Hamlet who can fly into the most shattering of pets.' Five years later (Lyceum) 'One's impression of this brilliant performance does not outlast the moment of its brilliance. It is cometary. That was Hamlet, that was! and the sky is empty again.' It gives me the greatest pleasure to say that now at last Mr Gielgud has stopped all the gaps.

The too-young Hamlet takes one's thoughts off this play in the way that the concert-hall's infant prodigy takes them off the music: one fritters away attention wondering how all those runs and trills have been managed. Mr Gielgud is now completely and authoritatively master of this tremendous part. He is, we feel, this generation's rightful tenant of this 'monstrous Gothic castle of a poem.' He has acquired an almost Irvingesque quality of pathos, and in the passages after the Play Scene an incisiveness, a raillery, a mordancy worthy of the old man. He imposes on us this play's questing feverishness. The middle act gives us ninety minutes of high excitement and assured virtuosity; Forbes-Robertson was not more bedazzling in the 'O, what a rogue and peasant slave' soliloquy. In short, I hold that this is, and is likely to remain, the best Hamlet of our time, and that is why I urge Mr Gielgud to stick to the mantle of tragedy and leave lesser garments to others. For this actor, like John Philip Kemble, is not really a comedian. John Philip had the notion that by taking thought an actor can qualify himself for the lighter as for the more serious side of his art. This is not so. All the trying in the world would not have turned, say, Matthew Arnold into a dinner-table wit. It is the same with acting. Again, in Mr Gielgud's case, the old couplet comes to mind.

Whene'er he tries the airy and the gay,
Judgement not genius, marks the cold essay.

As a comedian our First Player has no warmth, whereas as a tragedian he is all fire. He lives up to G.H. Lewes's dictum: the greatest artist is he who is greatest in the highest reaches of his art. And that is why I conjure him to stick to those rôles which entitle his critics to stand up and say to all the world: This is a great actor.

James Agate
Sunday Times,
22 October 1944

THE TEMPEST

Magic and Spells

I have to admit that at times a stage Prospero has been less compelling than that other magician, John Wellington Wells. I have known actors, each looking like Miranda's great-great-grandfather, who have either intoned the majestic verse through a thicket of beard, or boomed like wind in a farm chimney. On these occasions I have felt sadly the onset of what Bottom calls 'an exposition of sleep' – this, too, though *The Tempest*, on the page, is a miracle of the poet's mind. Possibly Shakespeare foresaw that kind of Prospero when he put in so many verbal nudges to rouse poor wearied Miranda.

In fairness, it is some time since I met a really deadly Prospero. Sir John Gielgud, at Drury Lane – and how good it is to write those two names in conjunction! – is a magician worthy of the verse. His performance has a sculptural quality. This Prospero is not a fuzzy recluse. He is a man who has fought hard for his knowledge, the power of giving fire to the dread rattling thunder, and rifting Jove's stout oak with his own bolt. On this isle in the far-off seas Prospero has grappled long and fiercely with the forces of magic. He speaks with a noble austerity, and he bids farewell to his art as a man who has challenged and overcome. The last speech haunts us by its wistfulness: it is not just the final exercise in a set of sonorous set-pieces.

To watch Gielgud as he commands the stage of Drury Lane, and especially to see him as, in his turquoise cloak, he makes farewell before the ship sails, with fair winds, towards home where 'every third thought shall be my grave,' is to know the splendour of a true classical performance. This is, without self-consciousness, the grand manner. It seizes the heart and mind.

In sum, then, the developed night for which at Stratford, in the summer, I had hoped. There, in spite of Peter Brook's powerful imagination – and no director has more – the night had occasionally seemed tentative, even though it was as good a *Tempest* as I remembered. The opening, as it is now at Drury Lane, was managed finely from the moment the ship's lantern began its dizzying arc. It was like Brook, also, to see the possibilities of that usually botched scene for the shipwrecked king and courtiers, and to offer it as almost a Shakespearean discovery.

Good; but I found, during the autumn, that the production was not staying with me as a whole. *The Tempest* was still ten leagues beyond man's life. Today, at Drury Lane, we can declare that we have landed on Prospero's island. Here let me add that, though I understand playgoers who ask for a fruitful isle, a place of 'bosky acres' and of 'lush and lusty' grass, I do believe more easily in Peter Brook's caverns by a 'sea-marge, sterile and rocky-hard.' It is a world of elemental forces, fit home for the bold magic of Prospero.

Various small things have been altered for the better on the passage to Drury Lane. Ariel, if I recall, no longer uses his telescopic mushroom; Caliban's appearance is modified. Most important, the epithalamic masque is changed. At Stratford, with those white-robed goddesses, we had no hint of Iris, the 'many-coloured messenger,' and I was bothered by the dancers' reiterated fertility-rite chanting of 'barns, garners,' and so on. Now there is transformation. The goddesses are radiant. 'Great Juno' floats down upon a lazy cloud; and the moment when the grouped trinity is poised above the dancing nymphs and reapers is as 'harmonious charmingly' as we could wish.

Most of the performances are right, from the 'blest lovers' of Doreen Aris and Richard Johnson, who are simply in love, and who make no more ado about it, to the Gonzalo of Cyril Luckham, Robert Harris's movingly-voiced Alonso, and the Stephano (more and more Robeyesque) and Trinculo of Patrick Wymark and Clive Revill: quick, eagerly-defined clowns. The Ariel is still, for me, a loss – longingly I think of the work, so different and yet so satisfying, of Elsa Lanchester, Leslie French, Alan Badel – but the Caliban of Alec Clunes, though the actor cannot wholly smother his own charm, does keep the memory. I am unlikely to forget 'The isle is full of noises' which brings to us the sound and sweet airs, the thousand twangling instruments that hum about our ears. Mr Brook, with his much-discussed devices, has seen that the isle shall ring with strange sound. But I do wish that Ariel had a voice.

From the moment that Prospero and Miranda face each other across the great stage, as the ship vanishes in storm, this is a strange, exciting night: not, maybe, a *Tempest* for everyone – will there ever be a production with which all will agree? – but one absorbing both for its own sake and for its appearance on the stage of Drury Lane. This has been for so many years a theatre of more-or-less ephemeral flickers – though I would not for a moment deny my own pleasure in some of the nights – and it is a joy to hear the voices of Gielgud, Harris, Clunes. I wonder how many, at the première, were thinking of another *Tempest* on an evening in the autumn of 1838 when, as the wild storm faded, the Prospero of William Charles Macready descended a flight of rocky steps with the Miranda of Helen Faucit behind him.

J.C. TREWIN
Illustrated London News,
5 December 1957

PROSPERO'S NOVEL MASQUE

The Tempest

National

It is, of course, a special occasion: Peter Hall's incoming production as Director of the National Theatre; and John Gielgud's fourth Prospero, certainly his last on the stage where he played it twice before the last war. *The Tempest* itself, that serene ritual of reunions and farewells, matches the occasion; although before the eyes mist over with sentiment one notices that there is virtually no link with the National Theatre's own past; most of the actors are newcomers.

Inaugural flourishes apart, there remains the question of theatrical purpose; the reason for launching the National Theatre into its new phase with a play which is invariably belittled in performance. Mr Hall has an answer to that. He has approached his elusive quarry in a way I have not seen tried before. *The Tempest* is famously Shakespeare's response to the Jacobean masque. Productions customarily confine this to the passing details of the magical banquet and the nuptial visions. This version encases the entire work in a frame of masque-like artifice, which Prospero supervises in the role of a sublime stage-manager.

One advantage of this method is that it separates the production from its star.

At this stage of Gielgud's career it would be impudence on the part of any director to tamper with his reading, or involve him in personal concessions to an experimental scenario. But on John Bury's stage – a raised disc with an upstage promontory, and descending to floor level for the entrance to the cell – Prospero can control and view the action from outside, keeping his own tempos and long-studied inflexions in isolation from the shows he conjures up.

The masque element appears to be a straight continuation of Mr Hall's exploration of baroque opera. To start with, artificiality is underlined with wafer-thin trees smothered in leaves like sequins and an orange sun suspended on two visible cords. Costume is extravagantly courtly, with plumed head-dresses and helmets. The banquet is served by an awesome retinue of spirits sprouting multiple heads, limbs, and genitalia (the extraordinary work of Jennifer Carey). And when we reach the nuptials, a broken rainbow descends and the piece passes right over into opera as Iris delivers her prologue in melismatic recitative to a drone accompaniment. Music, by the Gryphon group, mingles medieval dance (with growling reed instruments) and Indian pop; very stately and discreetly turned on.

The baroque novelties culminate in Michael Feast's Ariel: an androgynous factotum, descending from the flies on a bow-like trapeze, sometimes in gnarled claws as the harpy, or in flowing hair as the sea nymph, and rising into a penetrating counter-tenor for the songs.

The atmosphere, in short, is heightened in a spectacularly formal way that runs in parallel with the elevation of the poetry. Shakespeare's natural breathing has to keep pace with a tightly schematized style. And it seems to me that the production has not faced the main question of the play: whether *The Tempest* represents a challenge to the masque, or an effort to digest it; whether verbal imagery can still survive in a world of dazzling physical imagery.

So far as Gielgud is concerned the question does not arise as he stands outside the stylistic framework. The part is peculiarly his own property in the sense that the character of Prospero resides in its verse rhythms; and no other actor is so well equipped to handle those huge metrical paragraphs with their abrupt contractions, and extensions of imagery almost beyond the bounds of syntax. There are some surprises. 'Our revels now are ended', is delivered urgently and at speed. The passage is one of the part's insoluble problems; as Prospero is in danger, and yet the poetry invites lingering attention.

But in general the performance is as I remember it from the 1957 production: aloof, immeasurably elegaic, with the suggestion of internal struggles remote from the surrounding drama. For the epilogue Gielgud removes his wig, and steps out of character to speak simply as an artist addressing his public.

The other performances fall into two groups: and, significantly, the comic are by far the more vital. It would be going too far to say that Julian Orchard and Arthur Lowe succeed in making Trinculo and Stephano funny; but they do bring them unusually to life. Mr Orchard, a fleshy ladylike stooge in cap and bells, and Mr Lowe, a dangerous buffoon with a powerful sense of his own dignity, make something very real of the subplot; and their enslavement of Caliban is genuinely disturbing.

Denis Quilley's Caliban is the most original performance in the production. His makeup is bisected: on one half the ugly scrofulous monster whom Prospero sees, on the other an image of the noble savage: and as Mr Quilley plays him, he is striving to break from the first stage into the second. His delivery of the word 'freedom' even in the catch (which the three plotters sing in character) echoes with more passion and meaning than anything else in the evening. At this point, at least, Mr Hall has extracted real content from the play.

Elsewhere, the masque conquers.

There are a couple of quiet, insect-like villains from Cyril Cusack and William Squire. But Ferdinand and Miranda emerge as neutral dolls; the Court look magnificent and cut no ice. The spectacle is generally splendid; and, as Shakespeare's own contemporaries complained, hollow.

IRVING WARDLE
The Times,
6 March 1974

THE NATIONAL'S GREAT TEMPEST

There is only one word to describe *The Tempest*, Peter Hall's first production for the National Theatre, and for once it can be employed literally. The word is fabulous.

Fabulous, but not by any means fanciful: Mr Hall's approach is, by the lights of this play, scrupulously realistic. He begins with a thoroughly convincing storm, the hard-working, hard-lurching sailors beset by a bunch of troublesome courtiers scrambling up from a cabin below decks. At the close of the scene the roof of their cabin slams shut; standing on it, the first of a series of inspired transformations, is Prospero, the controller of the tempest and of the play.

His control is not, in John Gielgud's performance, serene or untroubled. To work magic on this scale requires of him an enormous effort of concentration; his magician's robe weighs him down and it is a relief to him to shed it. He lays great stress on the line about 'the most auspicious star' on whose influence, necessarily transient, his success depends. This Prospero is engaged in a race against time and this awareness colours the whole of his dispute with Ariel, whose demand for his liberty 'before the time be out' endangers the whole scheme.

As it turns out it is only when the scheme is successful that Prospero's real troubles start. For the time being his charms work like a charm. The responsibility for showing this is not the actor's (since Prospero has a habit of not being around while his spells are operating), but the director's, and Mr Hall shirks none of it. Some of his *coups-de-théâtre* are truly *coups* of grace: the appearance of Ariel as a water-nymph when we expect the lumbering entrance of Caliban (I know the play by heart and this moment still took me by surprise, so cunningly is it staged) and the arrival of Ferdinand on the spot where Caliban had stood only a second before.

This last trick is effected with the aid of sliding scenery. One of the prime qualities of the isle, as realised by John Bury, is its mobility: a theatrical delight to be relished as such. The masque element in the production erupts in two set pieces: the vanishing banquet, borne by 'strange shapes' like a bad baroque dream of fertility corrupted, and the show of goddesses, sung throughout (which I found excessive, but pardonable) with Iris perched aloft, somewhere under a rainbow.

All of these wonders are germane to the play; most of them are explicitly demanded by it, though few directors respond as generously as Mr Hall. His triumph in this vein is his treatment of Ariel; 'an airy spirit' he apparently *lives* in the sky (I said that this was a literal-minded production) whence he regularly descends by pulley. (I came to think of this contraption as Ariel's aerial.) Nearly always he is in some disguise; by his constant changes of shape Michael Feast comes as close to incorporeality as can be asked of any actor. He has besides two voices (which makes him, as Stephano remarks in another context, 'a most delicate monster'); he sings both tenor and counter-tenor, rendering in the latter the lovely original setting of 'Full fathom five.'

'But this rough magic I here abjure'; the effects can only furnish the groundwork of the play, and in the end everything depends on Gielgud. Approaching victory he approaches despair: 'Our revels now are ended' is savage rather than lyrical. His renunciation of revenge is tremendous, though not marked by any weighty pause. His tormented outburst against the 'born devil' Caliban is balanced at the end by a glimmering of tolerance; a tolerance more than deserved since Denis Quilley's Caliban, though resembling a Hiawatha who has gone berserk with the tomahawk and scalped himself, yet contrives to appear attractive. His roar of 'freedom' has amazing force (in every performance of Mr Quilley's there is one moment that makes me think him the most exciting actor in the world and this is it), so his abasement before Stephano is all the more poignant. Arthur Lowe's Stephano is as funny as you would expect and more than twice as mean; his function in the play is brilliantly illuminated in his final appearance in his stolen regal robes, to be greeted by Prospero's wry 'You'd be king of the isle, sirrah?' Suddenly the stage appears thronged with monarchs, true and false; not for nothing do mirrors feature heavily in Mr Bury's set.

One parallel stands out over all; in his ducal gown Prospero is a dead ringer for his usurping brother Antonio, who emerges, far more than Caliban, as the play's negative pole. The role has been unusually strongly cast with an actor, Cyril Cusack, who approximates to Gielgud's own stature; untouched by the forgiveness at the close (though when Miranda appears he looks as though he might be harbouring avuncular thoughts of rape), he breaks silence only to make a sour joke over Caliban. One glance between the brothers at the end establishes them as eternally unreconcilable.

Having absorbed both this blow and his effective desertion by Ariel (who, having finally gained his freedom, celebrates by taking an express lift upstairs), Gielgud speaks the Epilogue, and sets his seal on the role forever. His next appearance (in Edward Bond's *Bingo*) will be as Shakespeare himself. It seems logical.

ROBERT CUSHMAN
Observer,
10 March 1974

APPENDIX II

The Hamlet Tradition

Some Notes on Costume, Scenery, and Stage Business

BY

JOHN GIELGUD

(Written in 1937)

Ellen Terry describes Henry Irving's appearance as Hamlet minutely in her memoirs, and speaks of it as if it were revolutionary and original at the time – 1874, when he produced *Hamlet* at the Lyceum. The pale face, disordered black hair, simple tunic edged with fur. 'No bugles, no order of the Danish Elephant – he did not wear the miniature of his father obtrusively round his neck.' Perhaps she is thinking of Fechter, who played Hamlet with Ellen's sister Kate (my grandmother) as Ophelia. He was a fair Dane, and a print I have of him in the part certainly looks as if his costume was elaborate, though vaguely Nordic and barbarian.

If Irving's Hamlet broke one tradition, it certainly started another, which has varied but little in Continental or American representations of the part from that day to this. Of an earlier date is the famous portrait by Lawrence, of John Philip Kemble, with his hat of plumed feathers and long cloak. There are interesting prints of Macready, Forrest, and others in which the miniature is usually predominant, if not the bugles. Following Sir Henry, his son H.B. Irving naturally copied his father's make-up and costume, and looked extremely like him. Forbes-Robertson, who had played continually with Irving, also wore much the same attire. Booth wore cross-garterings instead of plain black tights. Salvini, Moissi, Katchalov, Kainz from the Continent – and, of course, Sarah Bernhardt; Booth, Sothern, Hampden in America; and in more recent times, Tree, Wilson Barrett, Ainley, Barrymore, Martin-Harvey, Milton, Swinley, and Tearle – all these famous Hamlets conformed more or less to the traditional appearance of the prince. Tree wore a fair wig and beard, in which unkind people said he looked like a German professor, and Wilson Barrett was extremely *décolleté*. Basil Sydney in America, Colin Keith-Johnston in London, and Moissi in Vienna, played the part in modern dress.

A production done in England in sixteenth-century costume which made a stir was that of the late J.B. Fagan at Oxford in 1924. This was an amateur performance by the Oxford University Dramatic Society in which Gyles Isham made a great success as Hamlet. The costumes were of the Dürer period, and the men wore puffed sleeves, short surcoats, and slashed tights. The Ophelia was not assisted by a hat with a very long and ridiculous feather (in the play scene); otherwise the costuming was strikingly effective.

The late William Poel presented *Hamlet*, among many other Shakespeare plays, in Elizabethan dress. His first experiments were as early as 1881. An even earlier attempt was that of Benjamin Webster at the Haymarket in 1844. Since Poel's productions, the method has been followed at the Old Vic and elsewhere on various occasions. The first time I played Hamlet (1929) at the Vic, Harcourt Williams used this period for his production. The most practical drawback to it is that the women are not sympathetic dressed in farthingales, which seem to be stiff and ugly in an emotional or pathetic scene, nor are the men helped in tragic or exciting scenes by the short cloaks and bolstered trunks of the period. Besides, the actors find these clothes very hot and tight to act in.

The archaeological period – Saxo Grammaticus – which is the traditional theatrical and historically accurate period for the play, has the opposite disadvantage. The women look like virgin heroines from grand opera, with plaits, girdles, and straight dresses with key-pattern borders, and the men are hampered and made absurd by warlike studded breastplates, thongs and winged helmets, contradicted by skinny arms and smooth faces, or 'dreadfully attended' by voluminous wigs and beards. Gertrude and

'My lifelong ambition was to play Prospero on the screen.'
Prospero's Books, 1991.

Above: left: Cassio, w
Ion Swinley as Iag
and Ernest Thesiger
Roderigo, Apollo, 19
The first of many
caricatures.

Above: 'Looking lik
Dante, without a bea
Prospero in *The Temp*
Old Vic 1930. Wood
by Powell Lloyd.

Left: 'A civilised ma
an uncivilised coun
Hamlet, New Thea
1934.

ove: King Lear, Palace Theatre, 1955. With Anthony Nicholls as Kent and Claire Bloom as Cordelia.

Below: The Noguchi designs for *Lear* 'had more to with Euclid than Shakespeare.' With Helen Cherry (Goneril), Claire Bloom and Moira Lister (Regan).

Left: 'We took to each other immediately.' Peter Brook who directed *Measure for Measure*, Stratford on Avon, 1950.

Right: 'Her success with Irving in the play made me want to do it.' Ellen Terry as Beatrice in *Much Ado About Nothing*.

'A rewarding part.' Richard I[illegible] Queen's Theatr[illegible] 1937.

Above: Charles Laughton as Angelo 'prowling up and down the stage in a big black cloak,' with Flora Robson as Isabella, in *Measure for Measure*, Old Vic, 1933.

Below: *Richard II,* 1937. With Glen Byam Shaw as Mowbray (left), Michael Redgrave as Bolingbroke, and Leon Quartermaine as John of Gaunt.

'No doubt he put the rather unequal English company through their paces.' John Barrymore as Hamlet, Haymarket, 1925.

Above: Harcourt Williams, producer at the Old Vic, 1929-1933.

Main picture: Laurence Olivier as Shallow, Old Vic at the New, 1945.

Above: Richard II woodcut, Old Vic, 1929.

Main picture: Richard II, Old Vic, 1929.

Inset: Mercutio, *Romeo and Juliet*, New Theatre, 1935.

Main picture: 'A court at odds with itself.' Richard II, with Peggy Ashcroft as the Queen, 1937.

Left: Mercuti
in a duel wit
Tybalt (Geoffr
Toone), with
Laurence Oliv
as Romeo an
Glen Byam Sh
as Benvolio, N
Theatre, 193

Below: Romeo,
Peggy Ashcrof
Juliet, 1935

Lear, Stratford on Avon, 1950. With Alan Badel as the Fool.

Judith Anderson as Gertrude, Empire, New York, 1936.

Hamlet, New Theatre, 1934.

Right: Hamlet, Empire Theatre, New York, 1936.

Below: 'Something of a "Shropshire Lad" Hamlet.' Richard Burton as Hamlet, Lunt-Fontanne, New York, 1964. With Robert Milli as Horatio.

'He was 45 when h
played Hamlet in
London.' John
Barrymore as Hamle
Haymarket, 1925.

Hamlet, Kronborg Castle,
Elsinore, 1939.

'I copied Irving's entrance, with a sheathed sword on my shoulder.'
Macbeth, Old Vic, 1930, directed by Harcourt Williams.

'Impossible to stage in a realistic or spectacular way." *Macbeth*, with Syb Thorndike and Henry Ainley, Prince's Theatre 1926. Designed by Charles Ricketts.

Henry Irving as Macbeth, Lyceum, 1875.

Claudius are liable to resemble the King and Queen in a pack of cards, and Polonius, in a pale blue gown, very long beard, and white staff of office, is boring before he has even opened his mouth. The key-pattern is sadly echoed in the scenery, climbing around doors, pillars, and arches, and the furniture, in trying to be primitive, usually looks uncomfortable and lonely, in spite of the skins draped hopefully about. The period can be strikingly handled as in the recent *Hamlet* of Leslie Howard, which, I am told, was beautifully set and costumed by Stewart Chaney, but I have a very vivid memory of H.B. Irving's archaeological production – the first I ever saw. I suppose I was about twelve at the time, and it made an unforgettable impression upon me. In this performance, Ophelia, played by Lady Forbes-Robertson, was introduced, dripping, on a bier at the end of the Queen's willow speech, to make an effective curtain – a very favourite Edwardian device to gain applause.

To return to Hamlet and his clothes. There is no doubt that the traditional costume of the Prince is becoming, loose, and comfortable – three essentials for such a long and exacting role. Long hair is apt to be more difficult to wear on the stage nowadays than short, but otherwise the dress is admirable to look at and easy to act in. Personally, however, I have always had a feeling that it is almost too much steeped in tradition, and therefore I have never worn it in the part. I like the more definite lines of the sixteenth-century dress – which I have always worn. (With slight modifications – as my own production was set in 1520 and the one in New York in 1620!) I feel the Renaissance costume suggests the scholar, the poet, the prince, the courtier, and the gentleman; that it is more youthful and at the same time more sophisticated than the Gothic Peter Pan of the traditional theatre. Probably if I had ever played in the cooler and more comfortable Saxon dress I should change my opinion.

Modern commentators seem to think that much should be made of Hamlet's appearance and costume after he feigns madness. Mr Granville-Barker even thinks he should wear colours in this middle section of the play. This innovation has never, I believe, been tried, partly, perhaps, because we actors know that black is becoming and dignified, and partly because the sympathy of the audience towards Hamlet on account of his love for his father's memory would be jarred by such an emphatic deviation from mourning. There is also the practical question of effort. Hamlet is on the stage nearly all the evening, and a change of costume is an added labour for the actor. I have tried changing into a violet and grey travelling dress for the last Act, thinking it would be a great innovation, and no one even noticed it (this was at the Old Vic). As to the 'mad' scenes, it is dangerous to overdo a fantastically disordered appearance – and almost impossible, in any costume, to follow Ophelia's detailed account of 'stockings foul'd, ungartered and downgyved to his ankle', without distracting the audience continually. An old print shows one actor who attempted this – Henry E. Johnston (1777–1845). One stocking is halfway down a muscular leg – the other twisted about, but the expression on his face is quite calm.

Ophelia's costume in the mad scene presents another vexed question of tradition. Walter Lacy, Henry Irving's adviser on his Shakespearean productions, undoubtedly voiced Irving's opinion when he said to Ellen Terry, who planned a black dress for the mad scene: 'My God, madam, there must be only one black figure in this play and that's Hamlet!' So in Irving's production and many others before and since, we have the white robe, tousled hair, and generally conventional appearance of Ophelia, with or without her flowers, which would pass equally well for Margaret in the last Act of *Faust*. She has variously been played since in black, red, and yellow. Mr Granville-Barker thinks she should have a lute in the first half of the scene and in the second part herbs picked from the garden which she delivers to the other characters as at a funeral. It was apparently the Elizabethan custom to distribute them so and it would certainly be appropriate and effective. Played by an actress in an Elizabethan dress (but not necessarily a farthingale) carelessly worn and soiled with mud and dirt, her hair dressed wildly but not altogether loose, Ophelia might become a stranger and more poignant figure than she usually presents in theatrical usage.

Two other points in costuming. Now that audiences are intelligent enough not to feel that 'there must be only one black figure in the play', there is no reason why both Ophelia and Laertes both should not wear black for their father. Not only does this mark the similarity and contrast of the two revenge stories, but it is particularly effective, in my opinion, in the final scene of the duel, when the two young men stand pitted against one another, fighting to the death for a similar cause.

There is one other innovation of costuming, which I have never seen attempted on the stage, but which is suggested most strongly by the text. In the closet scene, the Ghost should appear 'in his habit as he lived', i.e. in a cap and nightgown – or some kind of crown and robe – in contrast to his warlike appearance on the battlements. I believe the effect would be a fine one in so domestic a scene, and that Shakespeare intended it. It seems to be an impossibility to design 'silent' armour for the Ghost, and consequently he is always dressed extremely vaguely and underlighted almost out of all recognition, and therefore cannot make the impression intended in any of the scenes in which he appears. I consider that this was a bad failing in my own production, as well as in every other I have seen or appeared in, and I commend it as one of the important details worth study and solution in any future performance of the play.

As regards scenery: it is important, of course, in this play, that the sense of pictorial richness and sensuous decadence of a Renaissance court should be somehow combined and contrasted with the feeling of a 'warlike state', where ghosts and horror haunt the battlements by night; where armies are marshalling for war, graves give up their dead, and a barbaric northern feeling of cold and grimness cuts across the luxurious court life of the murderous poisoner and his shallow Queen. A pretty big problem, this, for any scene designer and director. The unlocalised setting, originally conceived and devised by Gordon Craig, and carried out by him with varying success in Stanislavsky's Moscow production in 1911, has of course influenced later productions tremendously. There was a violent reaction against the old-fashioned settings; and in Martin-Harvey's production, in Arthur Hopkins's *Hamlet*, designed by Robert Edmond Jones for John Barrymore, and later in my own, the influence of Craig was apparent. The chief danger in these unlocalised settings is the temptation to use steps and platforms to excess. The groupings and static pictures are greatly assisted by this means, but audiences quickly tire of looking at actors continually leaping up and down stairs that lead nowhere. Again, the solidity of such settings enforces a minimum of variations. If the interiors are impressively majestic, the scenes of the battlements and the graveyard are seldom equally convincing. Finally, the necessity of using drop curtains, near the front of the stage (in a totally different stage convention) for short scenes during which furniture is being moved on the main stage, is most unsatisfactory.

ACT I[1]

SCENE 1. THE SENTINEL'S PLATFORM BEFORE THE ROYAL CASTLE

(ACT I, SCENE 1)

This, one of the finest and most famous of all Shakespeare openings, is usually unimpressive on the stage. There are many technical reasons for this. Audiences will not be punctual, and, knowing the play well enough to remember that the principal characters do not appear until the second scene, fidget inattentively and do not encourage the atmosphere the actors need. In order to help the appearance of the Ghost, the stage is usually very darkly lit, and the scenery is either a drop-cloth, to allow of an easy and quick change of scene, or else a permanent set, which the producer bathes in deepest shadow, so that it may look different when used as an interior a few moments later. In addition to these drawbacks, the actors are all 'small part' men, with the exception of Horatio, and seldom capable of expressing by their voices and emotional power the great range and quality of the poet's invention.

The scene has been played high on a rostrum, down on an apron close to the audience, with wind, bells, clocks, twinkling stars, and music to heighten the effect. (The cock-crowing, by the way, which I tried in my own production, had never to my knowledge been used before, and was remarkably atmospheric.) But the

1 These notes are arranged according to the scene sequence of the London and New York productions. The act and scene notations given in parentheses are those of the standard editions of the text.

tremendously dramatic and staccato opening, the dramatic rhythm of the scene as it varies so markedly between the two entrances of the Ghost and moves towards its beautiful and poetic close – these beauties have not been apparent in performances I have seen.

With one exception. The production – in German – in which Alexander Moissi played in London in 1929, was, I believe an old one, originally Reinhardt's. The company was not of outstanding excellence, and there were many strange and ineffective innovations, but this opening scene was played better than I have ever seen it before or since. On a flat stage the soldiers waited, warming their hands over a brazier of coals. They were not raw young actors, but old and bearded veterans, whose terror at the sight of the martial figure of their old master, coming from such simple men of obvious physical hardihood, was moving and convincing in the extreme. Their trust in the wisdom of the young student Horatio seemed real and probable – he was cleverer than they and would interpret their fears. The disturbed feeling of imminent wars and of unseen horrors lurking about the castle, communicated itself immediately to the audience, and when Horatio spoke the famous lines about the dawn, his own relief and its effect upon the other actors made one feel as if a great curtain of darkness which had hung over them all during a long sleepless night had rolled away at last to let in the fresh air of the cold morning and another day.

One wonders how this scene can have been played effectively when it was originally written: a noisy fidgeting, mostly standing audience, no darkness, afternoon sunshine streaming on to a tidy little platform. But then we must remember that to know the play beforehand is a great loss for us today. It cramps our imaginations and our enjoyment of the thrilling drama of the scene, while demanding at the same time far greater conviction in the playing of it. No doubt first-class actors and simple production (with enough light to see every expression clearly) is all that is really needed to make it as effective as it should be, and so seldom is.

Notes

'Who's there?' I wonder whether Francisco is not meant to mistake Bernardo for the Ghost.

The cutting of the long speech of Horatio which is customary in the modern theatre has the disadvantage of making the second entrance of the Ghost follow far too quickly upon the first, which does not therefore take the audience by surprise as the author seems to have intended.

'I'll cross it though it blast me.' Horatio sometimes moves across the path of the Ghost on this line; alternatively he holds up the cross-hilt of his sword and makes a cross in the air with it towards the Ghost.

SCENE 2. THE COUNCIL CHAMBER IN THE CASTLE THE FIRST SOLILOQUY; THE SCENE WITH HORATIO AND THE SOLDIERS

(ACT I, SCENE 2)

Commentators seem to agree that this scene represents the first privy council meeting held after the accession of Claudius as elective King. The more traditional stage usage has always been to place it in a throne-room or 'hall of the castle' with the monarchs on their thrones, a crowd of soldiers, ladies and attendants, and Hamlet seated on a stool apart or standing sadly below the chairs of state. Henry Irving, in stricter obedience to the text, had a long procession, at the end of which came Hamlet. Ellen Terry says, 'The lights were lowered at his entrance, another stage trick'; but this must have been cunningly contrived, and seems rather a curious artifice to resort to so early, in a play which is often hampered in performance by too many dark scenes. On the other hand, I once saw a Hamlet who made a 'star' entrance, centre, just before his uncle's first line to him; this made his first aside a little unconvincing, to say the least of it, and as he was also accompanied by a burst of limelight, he evidently thought differently from Irving.

In Barrymore's production, by Arthur Hopkins, the curtain rose in darkness, and sibilant whispering and laughter opened the scene, until the court was discovered lolling in amorous groups on a stage built up in masses of steps and at the top of them a great curtained arch. This first effect was most impressive, but the setting remained unchanged throughout the play, and the steps and arch became monotonous when used in many scenes.

Harcourt Williams, in his Old Vic production (1929) had the Queen and her ladies sewing and the King entering in cloak and gloves, as if from hunting. This was original, as well as being alive and vigorous.

The design of Gordon Craig for his Moscow production with Stanislavsky in 1911 has been often reproduced, and I have always been greatly impressed by it. Hamlet is sitting wearily in the foreground by a dark pillar. He is separated from the court by a barrier of mysterious shadow which cuts across the front of the stage, embracing the slight figure of the Prince. Beyond rises a brilliant pyramidal group of heads growing to a peak formed by the figures of the King and Queen, wearing huge cloaks, the folds of which seem to envelop the whole court. Actually at Moscow I believe the actors representing the courtiers put their heads through holes in the cloak (Komisarjevsky employed a slightly similar device recently in the trial scene of his Stratford production of *The Merchant of Venice*). How the exit was managed as the scene progressed and the cue was reached I have never been able to discover, but the drawing is extraordinarily dramatic and right in feeling, though it seems to me to be an idea rather than a practical stage arrangement. What attracts me most in it is the placing of Hamlet, the contrast of light and shade, and the focusing of attention on the King and Queen at the rise of the curtain.

I followed this scheme of grouping in my own production in 1934, but at an angle to the audience instead of straight, with courtiers ranged in a semicircle before the thrones and hiding Hamlet from his mother and uncle. The exit of Laertes caused a slight change in the positions of some of the courtiers and opened a space through which Claudius became suddenly aware of the presence of Hamlet. Then as Hamlet spoke his first lines the courtiers naturally turned to look at him, and the scene continued as the Queen came down from her throne to speak to her son, turning the whole focus of grouping and attention, at the right moment in the scene and not before, to the other side of the stage and to Hamlet himself.

Guthrie McClintic (in New York in 1936) placed the scene in a council chamber, and the King and Queen were seated behind a table. The court left the stage before the King addressed Hamlet, and the scene thus became a domestic argument between the three principal characters. This had a certain effect of concentrated development of the story, but I cannot help feeling that the formality of address used by Hamlet, and the flowery tone, half rebuking, half avuncular, of Claudius's speeches have greater point and effect when uttered for the benefit of his admiring and sycophantic courtiers. There is also a legitimate stage effect in a 'grand exit' at the departure of the King and Queen (and perhaps a 'grand entrance', too, as the scene begins). They can sweep from the stage to music and trumpets, the courtiers bowing and curtsying before they follow, until the solitary figure of Hamlet is left alone on the big, empty stage looking bitterly after them as he begins his first soliloquy. I think, however, that the privy council treatment, done more elaborately, with other councillors and officials, like Polonius, sitting around the table, might be very admirable.

First Soliloquy

I find this the most exciting of the soliloquies[1] to speak, partly because it seems to set the character once and for all in the actor's and the audience's minds, and partly for its extraordinarily forthright presentation of information as to the whole plot, matched unerringly in the march of the words and the punctuation of the sentences. Executed correctly it has no possible pauses except at the natural places marked for taking breath or when there are full stops. A short break seems to be demanded before 'Frailty, thy name is woman,' and another more definite one before the last two lines, which sum up the whole speech. Otherwise thoughts and exclamations succeed each other in the most vivid and natural

1 In this speech I very much wished to use the word 'sullied' for 'solid'. It is now agreed upon by most of the commentators as the correct reading, but fearing I should be accused by the ordinary playgoer, either of altering the line because I am thin, or else of pronouncing 'solid' with an Oxford accent, I gave up the idea. 'Faint and scant of breath,' in the last scene, has luckily been blessed with academic warrant as well as physical appropriateness in my own case.

manner, so that it is impossible to falter either in speaking or thinking. One is driven on at a naturally steady pace – in spite of a certain intensity of feeling which at first makes one tend to dwell upon some of the lines at greater length than others.

The following scene in which the soldiers come with Horatio to tell Hamlet of the Ghost has always been my favourite in the whole play, and I knew every word of it by heart long before I dreamt I should ever have the chance of playing the part myself. I also knew by heart the vivid description in Ellen Terry's memoirs of how Irving played it, and tried to follow him in every detail from the first. It may seem lazy for an actor to copy 'business' or readings from other actors, but I do not believe that one should ever discard tradition without first examining its purposes and inspiration.

Quite recently, in London, I saw a production of *Julius Caesar* in which the murder scene was improved by a 'curtain' in which Calpurnia was discovered kneeling – in heavy mourning (which she must have ordered very quickly) – at the side of her husband's corpse! This business had been invented by Tree, who was famous for such touches of originality. (At the first rehearsal of his *Othello* he is supposed to have said to Roderigo – Ernest Thesiger – 'We enter at the back in a gondola – and I thought it would be effective if you were hauling down the sail'!) Unfortunately, audiences love striking pieces of business and showmanship, and remember them long after they have forgotten the play in which they occurred. In Shakespeare, when they are pictorially attractive to the audience and make a personal effect for the actor too, they are difficult to resist. Irving was a great actor, and people who saw him will tell you that he was a genius at this kind of thing, and used it sincerely, originally, to the best advantage; but all the stars who followed him, particularly Tree, tried to outdo him in their lavishness and inventiveness. Irving's famous invention of Shylock's return over the bridge after the flight of Jessica – Irving, I believe, never actually reached the door before the curtain fell – has been copied and elaborated out of all recognition. Shylocks have knocked once, twice, ten times, rushed in, rushed out again, cried out, called through the house, rushed off down the street in pursuit. Tree topped them all by finding a handy pile of ashes on the doorstep and pouring them on his head. Nowadays if the Jew does not return at all when the scene is played, people ask why the great moment has been cut. It became the 'star' episode of the part because it was conceived by a fine star actor – and Shakespeare never meant it to occur at all!

Invented business such as this is obviously an interpolation. Audiences love it, but it is a bad concession to the picture stage and falling curtain, which Shakespeare never imagined, and underlines and elaborates a situation which the dramatist purposely touched on very lightly – and today it smacks of the 'problem picture' so popular in the Royal Academy exhibitions of twenty years ago. Therefore, there is little or no excuse for borrowing it or for inventing similar business at the same point in the text, though I am sure if I had seen it when Irving himself did it for the first time, I should have admired it as part of his invention, and, magnificently carried out, it must certainly have contributed to the brilliance of his performance as Shylock.

But when I read how, as Hamlet, Irving greeted Horatio, warmly but still abstractedly, still in his dream when he said 'My father, methinks I see my father——' how he half heard Horatio's line 'My lord, I think I saw him yesternight——' the dawning of intelligence on 'Saw. Who?' breaking into flashing realisation as his face blazed with intelligence from 'For God's love, let me hear!' – on to the quick doubts and suspicions in his questions and the touching appreciation of their loyalty as he said farewell to his friends – then I find a guide to the playing of the scene which seems to me still so perfect that I have never veered a step from it ever since I first rehearsed the part. Ellen Terry says that at the last couplet of the scene,

> . . . foul deeds will rise
> Tho' all the earth o'erwhelm them, to men's eyes,

Irving's acting appalled you by its implication of rising rage and horror, and this description, too, helped me to realise how those few short words bind the end of the scene together. The understatement of the court scene, the dull bitterness of the soliloquy, the rising excitement of the scene with the men – all this is caught together in the final words and leads the actors and audience unerringly towards the subsequent revelation of the Ghost and the setting in motion of the whole machinery of the action of the play.

I am always glad that we have few actual records, in films or gramophones, of the great actors of the past, though this feeling may seem to run contrary to what I have just said of the inspiration given me by the description of Irving's performance. I cannot help thinking that the greatness of all fine acting lies to some extent in its momentary creation, before an audience – that the inspiration (and the 'copy' of the inspiration which in many consecutive performances actors give by means of what they call technique) is partly contributed and guided by the audience present at any particular performance. The effect of an acting moment may be one of unforgettable vividness, but it passes immediately and merges into another, which the actor has carefully prepared and arranged so that his performance may proceed harmoniously and in a certain line with his development of the character and the progress of the play's action. Afterwards the spectator may remember and record certain vivid impressions, but probably if he goes again to see the same performance – indeed, even if he sees rehearsals and watches a performance every night – he will never again receive exactly the same impression. The temperament of the actor must vary, to a greater or lesser extent, according to his own mood and the mood of the other actors and of the audience.

But, just as a great teacher trains his pupils to adopt a correct method of study, and leads them towards the most sincere approach to an appreciation of style, so, it seems to me, an aspiring actor should be able to study these essentials from watching his masters in the craft. It is not from a great actor's mannerisms, or some brilliant but fundamentally personal expression of voice, gait, or carriage that he will learn, but from the master's approach to character, and from every moment in his performance in which he reveals or clarifies the text. These moments, I am sure, are only evident to one who has actually seen a stage performance. A great actor, even if he is not playing his best, is more interesting to me 'in the flesh' than his shadow, however well made up and lighted; and his voice, however husky, or even bored, has more life in it than a reproduction, no matter how cunningly reproduced by machinery. The mechanics of cinema and gramophone advance too quickly. The films and records of Bernhardt and Ellen Terry are ridiculous and inadequate curiosities today – and who knows that future generations will not laugh at the records of Caruso and Chaliapin and the plangent masks of Garbo, Dietrich, and Gable? Some idea of an actor's performance may be conveyed to a third person by a brilliant and expert description or critique, written or told by an eyewitness, but I do not believe that any mechanical reproduction can recreate an acting performance that one has never seen (though it may be an interesting reminder or a valuable curiosity) whereas a description may suggest it most vividly and encourage those who come after to use it creatively without any spirit of imitation.

Hamlet is, of course, the greatest play of tradition in our language. Nearly all the great players (and many not great at all) have attempted to make history in it by touches of originality – from Garrick overturning the chair in the closet scene to Edmund Kean kissing Ophelia's hair, from the death shield of Forbes-Robertson to the plus-fours in Sir Barry Jackson's production in modern dress. I see no possible harm in reading about all these traditional or sensational innovations, and borrowing or discarding them as they seem to fit the character, the play, and the meaning of the text, as long as one does this sincerely and without losing sight of one's own original study and characterisation. It is curious to find, however, that the fuller the text used the less is it necessary to waste time resorting to business to illustrate the meaning or clarify the effect upon the stage. On the other hand, business has often to be invented by actors to cover the gap in thought made by a bad cut; often it takes no longer to speak the cut line than to carry out the business or make the pause that replaces it.

Tree, in trying to rival Irving's method without such good taste, and rearranging the text to allow of sumptuous tableaux and pageantry, found it necessary to cut extensively. The Victorian editors had already done their worst by publishing versions of the play ridiculously bowdlerised, and with long and inaccurate descriptions of scenery of which Shakespeare never dreamt. Tree was an eccentric character actor, and relied on brilliant make-ups and stage effects far more than on any real interpretation of Shakespeare. He and others started a fashion for hearty laughter, back-slapping, worked up entrances and effective curtains, which substituted pictorial show and business for real dramatic speed and the marvellously dramatic contrast of scene against scene, which lasted until the Granville-Barker productions just before the War.

Remnants of this style of Shakespearian acting have survived with some actors right up to the present day. The picture stage with its curtain, the effectiveness of scenery, lighting, and incidental music went to the heads of the Victorian and Edwardian theatre managers, and their audiences revelled in them too. They responded gladly to the 'inexplicable dumbshows and noise' which Shakespeare knew they loved so well. Today we have much to be grateful for. The circus and the cinema can always be relied upon to out-herod Herod, and we are forced back, in the theatre, to the realisation that nobody looks at the scenery, however fine, after the first minute or two, but that acting – voice, characterisation, movement – interpreting a fine play correctly will still hold an audience enthralled for hours on end. More time and hard work at rehearsals are of greater use than masses of money spent on scenery and costumes, and a producer who can handle actors is more valuable than a pageant master. Granville-Barker, Robert Atkins, Sir Philip Ben Greet, William Poel, and others like them, have done immeasurable service in rescuing the text from the ravages of the star actor-managers, and proving in performance how amazingly Shakespeare catered for his stage with the limited means of presentation and for nearly every actor in his plays, even in the small parts, if they are given their proper importance by the director and acted correctly by the performers.

SCENE 3. POLONIUS'S HOUSE OPHELIA, LAERTES, AND POLONIUS (ACT I, SCENE 3)

Ophelia, as Ellen Terry has observed, only 'pervades' her early scenes, and they are therefore notoriously difficult both for actress and producer. Compare her first appearance with that of

Desdemona, who is talked of long before she appears, so that the audience is impatient to see her, and whose strikingly gracious entrance on to a stage full of men is such a beautiful moment in the Senate scene. Cordelia, too, is a lonely and unforgettable figure – almost like Hamlet – in the great scene at the opening of *Lear*, and when she speaks for the first time, the whole interest concentrates upon her immediately. It is not so with Ophelia. Too much else has to be set forth in the first scenes of *Hamlet*. Though we meet her father and brother in the court scene, and they are marked for us in two or three telling little speeches, there is no mention of Ophelia until we see her, in a first scene which gives her little opportunity but to show herself to be an affectionate and charming sister and an obedient daughter. Both her first two appearances follow scenes of great dramatic power and emotion, and hers are apt to suffer by contrast. The audience is inclined to relax rather than stiffen in attention, especially as she usually finds herself in the modern theatre before curtains or a drop, and it always seems to me that the audience reacts to such scenes very much as children do. They attend with difficulty to what is going on in a front scene, knowing that something splendid is being prepared behind the curtain, and subconsciously longing to see what it will be. In spite of this handicap Ophelia's first scene is a justly famous and beautiful one, and makes a brilliant pendant, in its triangle of father, son, and daughter, to that of the uncle, son, and mother in the preceding scene.

Polonius is a grateful and rewarding part for a good actor, and has been played with conspicuous success with audiences since the brilliant performance of A. Bromley Davenport in the modern dress *Hamlet* of Sir Barry Jackson in 1925. Before this the part was usually cut extensively, and the admittedly difficult combination of wisdom and sententiousness was not appreciated or properly characterised. People are still confused by the speech of advice to Laertes with its worldly wisdom and moral precepts put into the mouth of the 'tedious old fool' and 'foolish, prating knave' of the later scenes. Davenport was the first to combine the elegance and admirably diplomatic manner of the court official with the selfish but strict attitude of a loving parent. This was his outward appearance. He used it to conceal his true character, which revealed itself as that of an inquisitive, pompous, spying old fox, who had surely bought his position with the new King by tactfully forgetting his allegiance to the old.

There has always been much speculation, particularly among actors, as to whether Hamlet and Ophelia were lovers before the opening of the play. Mr Granville-Barker has remarked on how useless it is to imagine that Shakespearean characters have lives apart from those they lead in the play. Though it is certainly true that we gain little by day-dreaming about the mothers of Desdemona or Cordelia, the question of Hamlet's relationship to Ophelia is very important to the actress who attempts to portray her – especially as Hamlet is too busy to mention the poor girl (even to Horatio) except in the scenes when he is actually confronting her. He makes sly digs about her to Polonius, and rants at her graveside, but in the soliloquies and sane moments, to his mother even, not a word.

The lines about conception and the fishmonger and the bawdy songs in the mad scene are the main reasons for supposing that Hamlet has been Ophelia's lover, but Dr Dover Wilson has explained the first, to my satisfaction at any rate, in his remarks on the entrance of Hamlet in his first 'mad' scene, of which I shall speak later. Mr Granville-Barker, however, does not take this view of the fishmonger scene, though he holds no brief for the lover theory. All we know for certain is that Ophelia says 'he hath importuned me with love in honourable fashion' and further that he has 'given countenance to his speech . . . with almost all the holy vows of heaven'. In the nunnery scene, Hamlet exclaims: 'I did love you once' and 'I loved you not . . . You should not have believed me.' Then he proceeds to rail at her as though she were a harlot, but it does not seem justifiable to make her one. If Ophelia is lying to her father in this first scene the effect of her lying to Hamlet in the nunnery scene is lost, and her innocence and purity as the thwarted ideal of his love spoilt entirely in its place in the play. As to the bawdy songs, psychoanalysis would nowadays seem to be so generally understood that any modern audience accepts them as the result of repression or wish-fulfilment rather than reminiscence. We are told that the purest woman often uses bad language under an anaesthetic. The Victorians and

Edwardians, who might have taken another view of the meaning of Ophelia's songs because of their own stricter upbringing, naturally never heard the lines, as they were always cut on the stage and often not even published in the books. Above all, for the purposes of acting and production, an Ophelia guilty of a concealed love affair is even more difficult for the actress to suggest than an Ophelia innocent of anything but the best intentions. The actress has a difficult task in any case, and nothing she has to do or say in this short scene, or indeed in any other, is clarified or explained by an interpretation based on her guilt.

SCENE 4. THE SENTINELS' PLATFORM: THE GHOST SCENE

(ACT I, SCENES 4 AND 5)

The two scenes on the platform should, I believe, be played together as they were in our New York production. The dropping of the curtain between them is most harmful to the continuity, and though the applause may be tempting, the difficulty of starting the following scene after the break soon dispels the charm of that. In the old days much play was made by the scene painters with a more remote part of the platform for the second part of the scene – cairns, gnarled trees, and Horatio's 'dreadful summit of the cliff that beetles o'er his base into the sea', were painted and built in detail. Leslie Howard played the scene in a crypt and Moissi by a large cross in a churchyard, which the Ghost leant on, looking like a very large turnip on top of a night-shirt (but rather terrifying all the same) growling out revengefully, while Hamlet sat on a step below, and jumped like a jack-in-the-box at the word 'murder!'

The difficulties of acting and production in these scenes are manifold. The Ghost must be unearthly yet revengeful, sad and yet inspiring, not too sorry for himself, nor yet too human in his resentment. I was not myself impressed by the much praised Ghost of Courtenay Thorpe, with Barrymore, nor have I ever seen the part played altogether to my satisfaction. In spite of the elaborate care with which he is described in the text, he is never dressed in full armour, and his vanishing is usually poorly contrived in a black-out. (But perhaps a successful effect by Mr Maskelyne might be distracting and sensational. One never knows.) I imagine that his disappearance down a trap – which would, I suppose, be laughed at by a modern audience – gave point, long lost today, to the lines about the 'cellarage' and 'old mole'.

In McClintic's American production, the voice was done with a microphone and loudspeakers, the actor being, of course, behind the scenes and another silent one walking on the stage. Though this was most effective for the first 'Mark me' and the 'Swears' under the stage (which often used to make the audience laugh in London, but were very impressive in New York) the house was quickly aware of the microphone device. It was impossible to hold the audience with it for long speeches, so later it was cut out and the lines spoken ordinarily from the wings. Even this was not as effective, to my mind, as a real actor would have been. He should, also, I think, be lit clearly and not over-disguised facially, as an audience cannot be interested in a mask-like face for very long.

Hamlet has a terribly difficult task in this scene, made twice as difficult by familiarity with the story, which robs the whole scene, with its purposely delayed climax, of half its effectiveness for actors and audience alike. The long speech on seeing the Ghost, which I have always spoken kneeling, is very difficult to build up with correct breathing, pace, and emphasis in the right places. It needs a good deal of voice yet must be somehow begun and finished with awe – and yet too much whispering in the dark hereabouts gets on the audience's nerves. The line, by the way, that got a safe laugh every night in the try-out in America was 'Something is rotten in the state of Denmark.' This did not seem very helpful for the scene, and so we cut it out. It is evidently a comic phrase to Americans!

I do not know how the tradition started of Hamlet saying 'O, horrible! O, horrible! Most horrible!' It belongs, of course, to the Ghost, and though I have taken it thinking to do something very effective with it, I have always regretted it afterwards, and would like to play with a Ghost who could utter it as it ought to be uttered. Irving is said to have made an impressive effect with it as

Hamlet, and could no doubt have made an equally great one if he had said it as the Ghost!

I think the main difficulty of the Ghost is the timbre of voice needed for the part. The scene is not usually rehearsed or played sufficiently in cooperation between the two actors. A director might, I think, get an extraordinary result by sound alone, but it is an impossible scene to play in and direct as well. It may be that I seldom please myself in it, and so I think it more ineffective because it is technically so difficult. I should like to see and hear Leon Quartermaine play the Ghost; he has to my mind the perfect voice for the part, combining dignity and sweetness with emotion and authority, as well as spiritual remoteness.

I have also an idea that it might be good to double the Ghost and Claudius – very effective, their physical likeness, from my point of view as Hamlet – but the qualities of voice and character needed for the two parts are so different that it would need a superb actor to differentiate between them without confusing the audience. Malcolm Keen read the Ghost's lines in New York and also played Claudius – but as he did not appear on the stage as the Ghost this was not quite the same thing.

I do not know whether I invented or acquired from someone else the business of seeing the Ghost from the expression of Horatio's face and then turning slowly and looking at it before 'Angels and ministers of grace', but I do know that this came off very well in London. For some reason I could not make it so convincing in New York. I have never written on the tablets, because I could not manage them and a pencil and a sword all at the same time. I have always used 'the table of my memory' and banged my head at 'So, uncle, there you are'. Schoolchildren always thought this funny, and I had to cut it (or do it very quietly) at matinées! I copied from H.B. Irving – not that I remember it myself, but read it in a criticism – the putting of my cloak round Horatio's shoulders at the end. I added to it by leaving my own cloak when I rushed from the men at the beginning of the scene (how actors have chosen to play such an emotional scene in a cloak throughout baffles me completely) and having Horatio put his around my shoulders because I was shivering. This is effective and not as elaborate as it seems in describing it, though possibly it falsely emphasises the 'curtain', when Shakespeare intended a quick exit, with the next scene following immediately. Effects of this kind, if not too elaborate, are to some extent, I think, demanded by a picture stage and descending curtain, though I fear we actors like them particularly because they bring applause more surely than a simple exit. When I directed a production of *Romeo and Juliet*, in which the front curtain came down only once, and one scene followed another in a different part of the stage – with even black-outs reduced to a minimum – I found it far less necessary to build up the ends of scenes with any device to encourage applause. Sometimes, indeed, several scenes would pass without any, and this certainly did no harm to the play, though unfortunately it always depressed the actors.

SCENE 6. THE COUNCIL CHAMBER IN THE CASTLE. HAMLET AND POLONIUS; THE ARRIVAL OF THE PLAYERS; THE HECUBA SOLILOQUY

(ACT II, SCENE 2)

When one studies and considers *Hamlet* through a great number of consecutive rehearsals and performances, one realises, perhaps, some of the things which account for its perennial popularity with actors and audiences alike. The scenes themselves are audience-proof. By this I mean that if they are played theatrically for all they are worth they will always hold the house. But audiences at this particular play are apt to be composed, either of people who know nothing of Shakespeare or of *Hamlet*, except what their parents and schoolteachers have told them, or else of students, scholars, and 'Hamletomanes', for whom every moment in the play is important, not only for its own sake, but for its significance with regard to the rest of the action and the psychological relation and development of the characters.

People who love the play and have studied it closely can frequently interpret motives in an actor's performance of the part of which he never dreamt himself. Conversely, with such a complicated character as Hamlet, the actor may try his utmost to present a certain meaning and yet never be sure that he has conveyed it clearly to the people in the audience, some of whom are admiring the poetry, some watching a pet theory of their own, some comparing the performance with others they have seen, some not attending at all.

The director, therefore, or so it seems to me, must take a very firm hand and do his best to help the actor to give and the audience to receive the same meaning at the important moments in the play. Perhaps this is to underestimate the average intelligence of the average audience, but all theatrical representation suffers when actors and audience are not properly fused; and in this particular play the fact already mentioned – that the scenes themselves are audience-proof – often makes it appear that this fusion has come about when really there is little except ordinary theatrical contact.

To develop this argument a little in relation to Hamlet's first appearance feigning madness: the lines with Polonius about the fishmonger and conception are archaic and to a modern audience vaguely connote rudeness, bawdry, suggestiveness, etc. But they will always be funny when spoken in the theatre (by which I mean they will get laughs and 'go' with an audience because the actors instinctively say them rightly, even if they do not completely understand them). Yet at rehearsals, actors and directors always try to reason out this scene. Dr Dover Wilson has evolved a clever theory that Hamlet's entrance should take place some lines earlier than when the Queen's 'but look where sadly the poor wretch comes reading' heralds his appearance. Both in my own production and Mr McClintic's I tried taking different cues for this entrance in the hope that Hamlet's overhearing the last lines of Polonius to the King and Queen would make clearer the lines in his scene with Polonius, as well as his subsequent treatment of Ophelia in the nunnery scene. One or two people noticed this treatment, but on the whole I do not think it clarified the meaning sufficiently to warrant the trouble we took with it at rehearsals. I was also afraid the audience might mistake my meaning and wonder what was happening (whether one had made a mistake and come on too early), and while they were speculating thus, miss what followed. I was continually struck with the feeling that if Shakespeare had meant Hamlet to overhear something in this scene he would surely have made it clear in the text. The play has much spying in it, and two or three of the most vital moments in subsequent scenes are built around that device, but in each case it is Hamlet who is spied upon. I think it unlikely that Shakespeare would weaken such a characteristic feature of his play by making Hamlet spy on, or overhear, any other character before the more important point of the spying of his enemies on him had been definitely registered with the audience.

Mr Granville-Barker draws attention to the long stretch in this part of the play in which the actual plot is never touched on at all. From the entrance of Hamlet until he says to the Player: 'Can you play The Murder of Gonzago?' the plot does not move forward. The variety of the dialogue and wealth of theatrical invention is so extraordinary that I had never noticed this important point, either in acting or producing the play. Reading Mr Granville-Barker's stimulating essay, I was greatly helped by his remarks, forcing myself to decide on certain definite moments in the scenes in which Hamlet must remember his mission of vengeance and is shocked to find how easily he has been forgetting it. Yet, though I tried to make these moments clear in my by-play, for an audience seeing the scene there is so much else for them to watch and listen to – so much beauty and wit, action and counter-action – that this point, so very important to the actor playing Hamlet, does not really matter greatly to the spectator.

I cannot quite decide in my own mind whether Hamlet asks the player emphatically for a passionate speech, thinking at that moment of his own lack of passion, or whether Shakespeare is simply writing towards his climax with unerring instinct, suggesting it in advance, as a composer might use a warning note before introducing a great theme in a symphony. I have been struck later in the play by the lines,

> . . . bless'd are those
> Whose blood and judgment are so well co-mingled
> That they are not a *pipe* for Fortune's finger
> To *sound* what *stop* she please,

coming only a little while before the scene with the recorder. This earlier passage seems to me something of the same kind. At any rate, Mr Granville-Barker has led me to much greater ease during the recital of the player's speech by his remarks on the subject. 'The unnerved father falls' must surely strike Hamlet as a vivid reminder of his own forgetfulness; and 'Aroused vengeance sets him new a-work' serves finely as the first point in his determination to clear the room and unburden himself to the culminating, 'O, Vengeance!'

I shall never forget the tremendous effect of this scene in the Moissi *Hamlet* of which I have spoken before. The First Player was, perhaps, the finest actor in the company – an enormously tall man, over six feet, with deep-set eyes and black hair and beard. He played the part as high tragedy, and at the end of the speech on Hecuba he veiled his face with the cloak thrown over his forearm and fell headlong on the stage. This was extraordinarily moving, and beautifully carried out. It showed, as usual, what can be made of the smaller parts of Shakespeare and how greatly it helps the central character when they are played, as they so seldom are, to the full extent of their possibilities. If the Player has done his work well, Hamlet's comments need only echo the audience's thoughts, and how much more moderately and easily they can be expressed than if Hamlet must 'tear a passion to tatters' to convince himself and the audience of something they have not really seen. In Moissi's production also, Hamlet left the stage at the end of the Hecuba soliloquy, and, as far as I remember, received just as much applause at this point as any other Hamlet. For some reason I have never been able to bring myself to do this, though, of course, it is what Shakespeare intended. I suppose I was hypnotised by the famous business of Irving, when, as the curtain falls, he is seen writing madly on his tablets. One cannot help feeling that

> The play's the thing
> Wherein I'll catch the conscience of the King

should be the signal for the greatest applause in the play. When I have played the part on first nights I have never been able to believe that I could succeed in it until this applause had come. At later performances, however, I have been, and still am, irritated by my actor's desire to make such a 'curtain' of it. If we could bury the play for twenty years we might perhaps feel it mattered less how certain parts of it would be received than whether the great speeches would be correctly interpreted in their own place in the play.

I have spoken a great deal in these notes about stage business and the Victorian and Edwardian traditions of Shakespeare which I deplore in the theatre. At the same time I know only too well that my own performance has been cluttered with these things. I have never been either sufficiently experienced or sufficiently original to dare to direct or play *Hamlet* without including a great deal of this kind of theatricalism, for fear of being unable to hold the interest of the audience by a more classical and simple statement of the written text. As in music, it needs the greatest artists to perform most simply and perfectly the greatest composition.

SCENE 7. THE GREAT HALL IN THE CASTLE. 'TO BE, OR NOT TO BE'; THE NUNNERY SCENE (ACT III, SCENE I)

I remember in the Moissi production when I could not follow the text because it was in German, that I was surprised by 'To be, or not to be' coming so quickly on top of 'O, what a rogue and peasant slave am I'. This contrast had never struck me before because there had always been an act wait between these two scenes, and then another before the play scene. When we first rehearsed the play at the Old Vic it seemed obvious that the best place to have the only interval was after the nunnery scene rather than before it. Apart from the time lapse which is suggested in the text there is also the practical consideration of preventing people coming in late and slamming down their seats during 'To be, or not to be', whereas, if they miss the whole of the advice to the players (which, however, is hellishly difficult to play in such circumstances), they will have lost nothing of the main progress of the plot.

Apart from this, I realise now that the effect of despondency in

'To be, or not to be' is a natural and brilliant psychological reaction to the violent and hopeless rage of the earlier speech. If it were not such a famous purple patch which everybody in the audience is waiting for all evening, it would seem perhaps more perfectly placed for the character than it does. I imagined I created a great innovation by walking about in this speech and was extremely proud of the way I slipped in the opening words, trying to make not too long a pause before them, and to get under way before the audience was quite sure it really was the big speech. But, of course, this defeated its own ends in time. When I did the play in New York I became self-conscious in the walking, and after a few nights Mrs Patrick Campbell, who came to see the play, implored me to cut it out, as she said that watching the movements distracted from the words and destroyed the essential sense of composure necessary for the full effect of the lines.

The familiarity of this scene is an utter curse. Several times a week one is distracted by the knowledge that the audience are repeating one's lines after one – frequently one can hear words and phrases being whispered by people in the front rows, just before one is going to speak them – indeed, Leica cameras and the quoting of famous passages aloud are two of my worst phobias in a performance of Hamlet. This particular speech in itself is such a perfect thing that if you have executed it correctly you are apt to feel complete and satisfied at the end of it, but not ready to go straight into the rest of the scene. Like so many other great speeches in this play, it has to be studied, spoken, re-studied, and re-spoken, until one can combine in it a perfect and complete form of poetry and spontaneous thought, and yet at the same time use it only as a part of the action. The character and the value of the speech lie in the fact that it leads on to the next part of the scene, just as it must grow out of the previous action. Of course, the better one speaks it and the more completely one can win the audience by a good delivery of it, the more easy it should be to join it to the subsequent conversation and interplay with the other characters.

The scene with Ophelia has never really been explained to my satisfaction in any book I have read or performance I have seen. I have never been able to decide positively for myself its general meaning or the particular meaning of many of the lines. I cannot be convinced by the traditional business of Hamlet seeing the King and Polonius before saying, 'Where's your father?', nor am I sure when Hamlet says, 'I loved you not', that he should immediately belie his words with affectionate by-play behind Ophelia's back. This is another of Irving's legacies which I inherited at an early age. (Moissi, by the way, took out a big white handkerchief to cry in before Ophelia even came on the stage!) It seems to me reasonable to suppose that Hamlet suspects from the very first that Ophelia has been set on to spy upon him. ' . . . Are you honest?' That is why I have been inclined to favour Dr Dover Wilson's theory of overhearing Polonius's 'I'll loose my daughter to him' in the other scene, though against this I feel that so much time has elapsed between the two occasions that I doubt if an ordinary audience seeing the play for the first time would notice the connexion.

'Why wouldst thou be a breeder of sinners?' has led some commentators to suppose that Ophelia might be pregnant, and bolsters the theory already discussed that Hamlet and she have been lovers. The prevalent opinion seems to be, however, that the idea refers to his mother. This applies also to the later reference to women painting their faces. The lines in which Hamlet accuses himself seem to me most poignant if they are spoken as if pleading with Ophelia to admit that she is not telling the truth. He is giving her every chance to speak out by showing her that he has just the same weaknesses as she. The scene is such an extraordinary mixture of realism and poetry that it needs elucidation. It maddens me to think that the author, were he here today, could so easily enlighten us as to the way it should be acted. The fact that like the other great scenes in *Hamlet* it is full of theatrical effect and is sure-fire with the audience does not make it any less of a problem both for the actor and director.

ACT II, SCENE 8. THE GREAT HALL IN THE CASTLE. THE ADVICE TO THE PLAYERS; THE PLAY SCENE

(ACT III, SCENE 2)

The advice to the players is always slightly embarrassing for Hamlet because he feels the audience is only waiting to catch him doing all the things he has told the players not to do. One of the most curious and amusing things about *Hamlet* is Shakespeare's mania for what one might call double suggestion. For instance, he invites an audience to watch an actor pretending to be a Prince apparently weeping real tears for his father, and a few scenes later he shows them the same actor being impressed by the mimic tears of another actor weeping for Priam's slaughter. He invites them to watch the actor who is playing the Prince discourse on acting and to see a play acted within a play. He asks them to mock at the damnable faces of Lucianus and the next instant to be thrilled by the terror of the King; to grieve with Laertes at his sister's grave, and yet to sneer a few moments later at the violent ranting of the two young men. The effect of contrast is echoed in the characters themselves – in the two sons avenging their fathers, the two princes waiting for their kingdoms, the two brothers, poisoner and poisoned, and the two women, shallow, weak, victims of circumstances, and tools of men stronger than themselves.

The question of the dumb-show and the whole content of the play scene has been most exhaustively discussed by Dr Dover Wilson. His views are fascinating, but I do not think that in carrying them out to the letter the conduct of the scene itself would gain, particularly for the average spectator. Well or badly played, well or badly cut, this scene has been and always will be one of the most exciting ever invented, although the great climax, 'Give me some light. Away!' has never been staged with any great invention. Presumably, in the Elizabethan theatre, the King and his court were brought on by attendants with torches. These retired during the action of the play, and at the King's cry they re-entered, and the court left the stage surrounded by this blaze of light, leaving Hamlet and Horatio alone. It is difficult to imagine that this was effective without artificial light, but perhaps torches flickering on the inner stage, which was out of the full sunlight, may have provided some illusion. Today fire regulations are so strict that it is extremely difficult to devise anything really effective with naked lights on the stage. They are not allowed either in London or New York, and a sore problem is added to the trials of the modern producer of classical plays.

Sarah Bernhardt is supposed to have snatched a torch from an attendant and held it to the King's face on 'What! frighted with false fire?', and Moissi did much the same with a large candelabra. Shakespeare, however, said, 'Suit the action to the word, the word to the action,' and as such fire is hardly false it seems a paradoxical gesture, though no doubt theatrically telling. Irving, I believe, created the business of lying on the floor with the manuscript in his hand, and of squirming on his stomach across the stage. He also played with a fan of peacock's feathers which Ophelia let drop, and which he tore to pieces as he lay exhausted on the throne, and flung away on the words, 'A very, very – pajock.' I do not know where the tradition originated of tearing up the manuscript – this has often been followed.

Macready, in this scene, waved a white handkerchief two or three times at the entrance of the King and the court. I have never been able to discover on what particular line he did it, but apparently it was a signal for applause from the audience in the same way as was the famous business of Edmund Kean in the nunnery scene when, having left the stage, he electrified the house by returning, tiptoeing across the stage, and kissing Ophelia's hair. (I always wonder how he accomplished this without her noticing it, and what she was doing while it was happening.) At any rate, it brought down the house. And so did the handkerchief business of Macready, until the American actor, Edwin Forrest, attended the performance one night, and hissed at this particular piece of business. Macready's diary is full of the incident and the rows and taking of sides which ensued on the subject, both in England and America. In the Tyrone Guthrie production at the Old Vic recently (with Laurence Olivier) the play was performed very clumsily by the actors, and the court reacted by laughing and mockery at various points. Opinion was greatly divided as to the effectiveness of this, but it seems to have held the interest splendidly, whereas in an absolutely uncut version it is usually inclined to flag. The Player Queen should, of course, be played by a boy.

The recorder scene was one of Irving's great triumphs, but many subsequent Hamlets cut it out. Personally, I would almost rather sacrifice anything else in the play, but admit frankly that the breaking of the recorder at the end of it – taken also, I think, from Irving, though I am not sure – is pure theatrical business and not justified by the text. Unfortunately I succumbed to it at the Queen's Theatre – not having done it originally at the Old Vic – and found the resulting applause, and chance of cutting several seconds playing time in a version that was inclined to run too long, too strong a combination to resist. When I played the soliloquy that followed, ''Tis now the very witching time of night', the scene would pass entirely without applause. This soliloquy, with its curious references to Nero and Hamlet's thought of matricide (never touched on anywhere else in the play), is one that does not 'go' with an audience – at any rate, when I have played it – any more than the following one of the King at prayers. Perhaps the speeches are too frankly Elizabethan in feeling, or it may be that they have less poetic appeal than others. In any case they are very difficult to deliver and unrewarding to play. Sir Philip Ben Greet wrote me that it was impossible to break a recorder, as it was then made in one piece, not screwed together like a modern flute. I replied, undaunted, that it was the most effective piece of business in the play and that people always liked it. I fear I am an inveterate ham, and shall never be the conscientious interpreter of Shakespeare that I should like to be.

In the Harcourt Williams production at the Vic, Polonius came with a candle, which I took from him, pointing with it to the cloud, which made the lines that followed frankly fantastic. I carried the candle through the rest of the scene, on into the King's room, and finally into the Queen's closet, where I set it down on a table. This gave a certain sense of continuity which I liked, but it did not fit into the stage management of subsequent productions.

It is extraordinary how the most obvious points of continuity escape one through familiarity with the play. I realised only the other day that, of course, musicians should play during the Gonzago performance and that the music they play must be pipe music. When Hamlet calls for more music to stimulate him after the excitement of the King's departure, the same musicians should reappear on the stage ready to play for him. Then he says, 'O, the recorders! Let me see one.' I don't think I have ever seen this done on the stage, obvious though it now seems to me.

Both Rosencrantz and Guildenstern, as well as Polonius, are frightened by Hamlet's behaviour at the play and anxious to get him to his mother as quickly as possible. I am sure it is this feeling of being hustled that makes Hamlet delight in ridiculing them and forcing them to leave him to come in his own time. The situation is a sort of pendant to the early part of the scene when they announce that the King will see the play and Hamlet hurries them off to summon the players. It could easily be stage-managed so that the audience would notice the excellent parallel stage effect.

I wonder, by the way, why the court of Claudius and Gertrude is always portrayed by actors representing young men and women. Gertrude must be nearly fifty, and in spite of the vanity of Queen Elizabeth, who certainly liked young people about her, it is surely more probable that a corrupt court under the influence of a king such as Claudius would include a great many older people. If I ever direct the play again I should like to have supers representing old councillors and ladies-in-waiting of about the Queen's age. The appearance of these in all the court scenes would suggest the complacent stupidity and mature decadence of Claudius's entourage. Hamlet, Horatio, Ophelia, Laertes, Rosencrantz, and Guildenstern would stand out by contrast as the rebellious young people of the play. It would also be a change to indicate that Polonius did not run the entire affairs of Denmark single-handed. On the other hand, the modern custom of casting a younger woman for Gertrude greatly enhances the effect of the part and the meaning of the story. In the old days, the part of Hamlet being usually played by older men, his mother naturally became the property of the 'heavy' actress in the company, and the result was not advantageous to the play.

SCENE 9. A ROOM IN THE CASTLE. THE KING AT PRAYERS

(ACT III, SCENE 3)

Mr Granville-Barker points out that the effect of this scene lies in the fact that the audience knows that Claudius cannot pray. Therefore, if Hamlet had known that the King was not in a state of grace he would have killed him. Of course this is brilliantly true. But how can it be shown to an audience and how can the scene be arranged so that Hamlet's long speech may seem natural and yet audible? I should like to try an effect which I venture to think may have been the one achieved in the Elizabethan theatre. Kneeling is, on the stage, a conventional symbol for prayer, but kneeling at a prie-dieu immediately suggests prayer itself. It seems to me that if the King knelt at the front of the stage on the floor and not at a prie-dieu or altar, and Hamlet appeared above (the upper stage of the Elizabethan theatre – a balcony or rostrum would serve the same purpose in ours) the kneeling figure would convey to Hamlet the idea that the King was praying, but the King's face, which the audience could see clearly, would belie the attitude of his figure. Hamlet could not actually reach Claudius without coming down on to the stage. His pause and subsequent speech would seem naturally to check him from doing this. He could then pass on along the upper stage, while the King would rise and speak his final lines, leaving by a side door. The inner curtains could then open to disclose Polonius with the Queen, and Hamlet would enter as if he had traversed a passage and descended a staircase – as he would actually have to do – behind the scenes.

Played as it usually is today before a drop curtain, the scene with Claudius is difficult for both the actors. Hamlet is so close to the King that, even when the words are whispered, the audience is aware of the falseness of the convention and think it very odd that Claudius does not hear. The sentiments of the speech are intensely Elizabethan and therefore do not appeal much to a modern audience. As Mr Granville-Barker says, the play is much more deeply concerned with what will happen to the individual after death than with any question of the momentary pain and violence of the act of dying. Today a lingering illness and the ugly attributes of the deathbed are what many of us fear the most, whereas the physical fact of sudden death must have been so continually present to the Elizabethans that they were inclined to consider the matter with greater philosophy than we do.

I am proud of a piece of business I invented in this scene – the only one, I think, that I can call entirely my own. I did not want to wear a sword in the play scene, as it is an impossible appendage to violent movement, but it is essential in the killing of

Polonius in the scene with the Queen. In London the sword was carried before the King in the play scene, and at the beginning of the following one he was seen taking off his crown and robe, but keeping the sword by him as if afraid to be left alone without it. Hamlet finds the sword lying on the chair, picks it up to kill the King, and at the end of the speech goes off with it in his hand to his mother. The King rises from his knees, finds the sword gone, and the discovery of its loss ends the scene on a legitimate note of excitement, and softens, to a certain degree, the rather trite-sounding rhymed couplet with which it closes.

Many critics believe that this scene is really the crux and climax of the entire play, but either because I have never felt that I played it effectively or that it was staged to the best advantage either in my own or other productions, I have not been able to agree with them. The following scene and the killing of Polonius is to me, as an actor, the climax of Hamlet's long inaction. The whole of the subsequent tragedy springs from this later moment. Besides, it is this physical act that seems to break the spell of doubt in Hamlet's mind and unloose his stream of repressed anguish and revenge.

SCENE 10. THE CLOSET SCENE (ACT III, SCENE 4)

It is a terrific strain to open this scene at the pitch at which the text demands, but it is essential to carry the mood of the play scene through the four or five scenes that follow it and maintain the feeling of a consecutive time-lapse. I realised, from a description of Bernhardt's cry: 'Is it the king?' when her sword was held above her head, making her whole figure into a great interrogation mark (as, I think, Maurice Baring has described it), the tremendous theatrical effect of the killing of Polonius, but the lines which follow have to be most carefully presented by the actors so that the audience may not miss the significance of both characters at this point. The Queen's line, 'As kill a king!' has to convey to the audience not only her horror at what Hamlet has just tried to do, but her dawning knowledge of what he implies Claudius has done.

Hamlet has to understand in a very few seconds, and convey clearly to the audience: (1) that he realises his mother did not know Claudius was a murderer; (2) that she set someone to spy on him behind the arras, and (3) that it is evident from her cry that it is not, as he imagined, Claudius whom he has killed.

I am constantly receiving letters asking me whether the Queen was an accomplice of her husband's murder. This is, I suppose, because the actresses who have played the part recently – Martita Hunt and Laura Cowie in London, and Judith Anderson in New York – have played her with real fire and sensuality, whereas in the old days, as I have said, she was played as the heavy woman – nothing more. It seems obvious to me, and I should have thought to everyone else (but one is never done with speculation in *Hamlet*) that Shakespeare meant her to be an adulteress, shallow, handsome, but not in the least wicked in the sense of being a murderess. Mrs Campbell said to me, 'The point about Gertrude in the closet scene is not that she didn't know Claudius was a murderer, but that she doted on him so much that she wouldn't have minded if he had been.' This seems to me feminine and shrewd.

The business of the pictures which, to judge from old prints was done at one period with portraits on the wall and later with miniatures around the necks of the characters, is another vexed point of theatrical tradition. Many recent Hamlets, myself included, have dispensed with both. But Mr Granville-Barker, to my surprise, advocates the miniatures. I suppose they are really warranted by the text, but I never dared to use them for fear that they would lead me inevitably to the elaborate business of dashing down Claudius's picture and stamping on it at the line, 'A King of shreds and patches!' This, I imagine, was the point at which Garrick knocked over the chair, which was supposed to be very effective. This is the point, also, where, it seems to me, the Ghost should appear in ordinary dress and not in armour.

The arrangement in New York was criticised in one case because Hamlet was between the Ghost and his mother. The Queen should be in the middle, it was said, to get the full effect of her inability to see the Ghost. On the other hand, if Hamlet is in the middle, there is a fine effect when the Ghost bids him speak to her and he addresses her over his shoulder with a movement of his arm, but still not looking around, his eyes fixed on his father.

The text seems to warrant a chair in this scene for the Queen to sit on, but I have always thought there should be a bed as well. In London we used curtains which hung in the middle of the stage, suggesting a bed. One half of the stage represented the King's room and the other the Queen's. The King knelt in prayer at one end of the bed and the Queen was discovered kneeling at the other. This gave a sense of atmosphere, but without too definite localisation. In New York we had a real bed (and no chair). I imagine it was very effective when I leaped on it and stabbed Polonius through the hangings, but, on the other hand, it was necessary for the Queen to sit on it, and, as somebody said, a Queen would never sit on a bed – it made her look like a housemaid! Another difficulty is that later, when the Queen is going out of the room and Hamlet begs her not to go to his uncle's bed, a real bed on the stage may encourage the audience to indulge in speculation as to the sleeping accommodation of the palace. This scene, and the scenes that follow, were probably most effective, and could still be played best, on an Elizabethan stage, with the inner stage arranged with hangings for the killing of Polonius, and the action in the scenes before and after it could then continue on the fore-stage, back-stage, and above, in quick succession.

SCENE 13. A PLAIN IN DENMARK. THE FORTINBRAS SOLILOQUY

(ACT IV, SCENE 4)

The scene with Fortinbras and his army seems certainly to require a change of scene, yet the modern picture stage fails, as usual, just at the moment when it should be most useful. A really effective setting might be possible with a revolving stage, but though we planned in London to use the entire extent of the permanent set for this one scene, lighted and angled at a different point from any other, we found when we came to the dress rehearsal that this particular arrangement was not good. We had to fall back on curtains as we did also in New York. Of course the soliloquy is most easily spoken close to the footlights, but it would still be of enormous value to suggest space, open air, and nature in the background after the madness and scurryings of the dark scenes in the palace. I did not see Chaney's Viking ship in Howard's production, which I am told was a fine innovation for this scene, but there is a drawing in Craig's *Toward a New Theatre* called 'Enter the Army', which I should love to see carried out in the theatre. If the audience could be somehow persuaded that they could see an army marching as clearly as Hamlet does, it would be a fine cross-current in the action of the play. But when one's mind begins to dwell on masses of soldiers and banners, one knows at once the danger of turning a production of the play into the kind of pageant that no doubt the pageant-master producers and Hollywood would be glad to make of it. If Hamlet is forced to conjure up in his imagination an army on the march, and succeeds in doing so, the audience may be readier to believe in its existence than if it were really there. I am told that Tyrone Guthrie arranged the scene brilliantly in his recent production at the Old Vic, with Fortinbras above on an eminence, in shadow, while Hamlet spoke on the stage below – and that Herbert Menges devised a brilliant effect with music to heighten the mood as the scene closed.

SCENES 14 AND 16. THE GREAT HALL. OPHELIA'S MAD SCENE

(ACT IV, SCENES 5 AND 7)

This is the point in the play where Hamlet at last gets ten minutes in his dressing-room, so perhaps I am not very well fitted to discuss it in detail. Once Ophelia has done her two showy pieces the house becomes inclined to polite indifference until the grave-diggers appear. But the King and Laertes have a difficult scene to play here which never seems to be very effective and is always severely cut, which probably does not make it any easier. And perhaps it is not possible in any play of Shakespeare's to avoid two or three stretches, usually in the fourth act of the standard editions, that are less interesting than others.

The Victorians often set this scene in a garden or exterior of some sort, presumably to help the idea of Ophelia's flowers and the Queen's description of her drowning. Needless to say, pastoral scenery is of little avail in illustrating Shakespeare's text. The entrance of Laertes with the mob is obviously more effective played indoors, and I am told it was one of the great successes of lighting and stage management in the Norman Bel Geddes production of *Hamlet*, in which Raymond Massey played.

Technically, the most difficult part of the scene is the entrance of the Queen to tell of Ophelia's death. Laertes' 'Drown'd! O, where?' has defeated many actors, and if the Queen is a good character actress she finds it difficult to fit the willow speech (as it is called by actors), which is a sort of cadenza, into the rest of her performance, to which it seems to have no particular relation. Here, I think, there is no doubt that a bit of the old grand manner is what is required. The actress must be given the stage and know how to take it, and not attempt to make a realistic effect with her lines. After all, if one examines it carefully, the whole situation is absurd, for if the Queen or anybody else had seen the drowning in such detail, something would obviously have been done to prevent it. Shakespeare merely uses the Greek Messenger method of describing an important incident happening off-stage, and no producer can hope to make the incident more convincing by arranging it realistically for the actress.

SCENE 15. HAMLET'S LETTER
(ACT IV, SCENE 6)

I have always retained the letter scene with Horatio as it gives some sense of continuity. The actor has a difficult time about this point in the play, for after being in attendance on Ophelia, we see him receiving Hamlet's letter, and then when we next meet him he is with Hamlet in the graveyard, knowing nothing of Ophelia's death. Here again it is no good trying to build the character too realistically in sequence. Shakespeare uses him all through the play in whatever way he wills, as a foil to Hamlet and the other characters, but he is so tactfully and rightly put in the foreground when Shakespeare needs him that the audience accepts him exactly as is intended, and believes all that he stands for in Hamlet's eyes.

SCENE 17. A CHURCHYARD. HAMLET'S RETURN; OPHELIA'S FUNERAL

(ACT V, SCENE 1)

Here a serious technical problem is presented to the scene designer. There is no time for an interval before or after – yet he must have a practical set, a grave, a glint of sky, besides some other suggestion of an exterior. Beerbohm Tree indulged in a spring landscape with blossoms, sheep scattered on the hills, and flowers which he picked for Ophelia's grave.[1] In the Reinhardt-Moissi production the scene was played at night by torchlight, and Ophelia carried on in white robes on an open bier. This was all very well. Unfortunately there was no trap, and, having set the bier above the grave, the men fought over her and were parted, the court retired, and poor Ophelia was left out all night for the daws to peck at, which seemed a little unchristian, to say the least of it.

A most impressive version of this scene was given in the modern dress *Hamlet*, for I suppose all of us (unless we are Irish) have a rooted aversion to modern funerals. The black, brass-handled coffin, wreaths, boots, and mourning-veils lent a sordid reality to the scene which I found quite unbearable. The gravedigger was, in this production, played by Sir Cedric Hardwicke, and he gave a brilliant performance on the lines of his old countryman in *The Farmer's Wife*. Ralph Richardson in another Old Vic performance also gave a memorable reading. The part does not seem to amuse

1 Also, no doubt, a formidable interval. I remember, too, the vivid description of Irving's first night in London as Hamlet, when Miss Bateman came on for the mad scene at ten minutes to twelve, and, with the rest of the play still to go, quieted a gallery already restive at the prospect of being shut out of the public houses for their last glass of beer!

an audience very much as a rule, but children love it and roar at the jokes and the business of the skulls, which seems rather surprising. George Nash, who was the clown in our American production, is certainly the best gravedigger I have ever played with. Without resorting to ten waistcoats or any of the old business, and with a very cut version of his lines, he contrived, as it seemed to me, to present a most Shakespearean and delightful rendering of the old fellow.

Hamlet and Laertes should surely not fight in the grave, for the moment they disappear from view it is impossible to see clearly what is happening, and the effect on the stage is bound to be ridiculous when they are separated and have to climb sheepishly out again. The lines do not really demand it anyway.

SCENE 18. A CORRIDOR. HAMLET AND OSRIC; THE CHALLENGE

(ACT V, SCENE 2)

Martin-Harvey, who played Osric at the Lyceum, says that Irving seemed to be surrounded by an aura of death in this scene. It is a very difficult passage to play, especially when the audience is flagging, and the actor out of breath from the rant in the graveyard which immediately preceded it. The necessary cuts always make one feel as if something had been left out, but even played in full there is an abrupt transition of mood and action. Again the necessary front scene demanded for the striking of the churchyard and the setting of the final scene cramps the actors for space and bores the audience, who begin to cough and look at their watches. The description of the pirate ship and the changing of the letters comes too late for the audience to be interested in it, and the actors always feel, however the scene is cut, that it is difficult to settle the house so that it will be attentive for the last stretch of the play.

A good Osric does much to remedy this, and I have been very lucky in those who have played the part with me – Alec Guinness in London and Morgan Farley in New York. Mr Granville-Barker has an interesting theory about Hamlet's attitude in this last part of the play, and I think there is much to be said for his suggestion that he should be keen, ruthless, his mind made up. But with this must be weighed the half-affectionate, half-philosophical mood of the scene with the gravedigger, of his words about Yorick, and his touching farewell to Horatio. These moments win such obvious sympathy from the audience that no doubt this is apt to encourage the actor at the end of a long part to play for pathos and sentiment more than he should.

The fatalistic vein in which he speaks, 'It is no matter. . . . A man's life's no more than to say "One". . . . If it be not to come, it will be now . . .' These are simple moments which, when spoken sincerely, will move almost any audience. But the general attitude of the character all through these last three scenes is extremely difficult to reconcile with the violent and often more showy passages in the earlier scenes, and the actor has to take the line which he feels is most justified by his reading of the text and his whole conception of the character.

SCENE 19. THE GREAT HALL. THE DUEL; THE DEATH SCENE

(ACT V, SCENE 2)

The final scene is apt to be a little ridiculous unless everybody concerned is very careful. Irving made his one really ill-judged cut in this play here, and left out Fortinbras altogether. The rest of his acting version is well arranged and compares favourably with his other Shakespearean texts which were maltreated and bowdlerised to a shameless degree.

Recent productions have made the fight tremendously pictorial and built the whole scene around it, especially in the productions in which Raymond Massey and Laurence Olivier played. As I am not a good swordsman, I have never myself attempted more than is absolutely necessary. Frankly, also, I haven't the energy for it at the end of such a long and exhausting part, but the better the fight is done, of course, the better for the scene, and if the stage can be arranged for different levels to be used for the duelling the effect is proportionately greater.

I have always fought with rapier and dagger as the text seems to demand. Moissi, to my amazement, after an elaborate but quite anachronistic eighteenth-century fight with foils (in a Gothic production) took the poisoned sword by the blade with both hands and stabbed the King in the back! The guards, in diagonally striped cloaks, then closed in three groups covering the bodies of the King and Queen and Laertes, making a background for Hamlet himself to die against. This was too much of a stunt, and I prefer my own arrangement of the scene, in which the Queen and Laertes died on big thrones, one on each side of the stage close to the footlights, and the King in a big cloak and crown was pursued up to a centre platform, where he fell in a swirl of red folds. There were still steps below for Hamlet and Horatio to play their final scene, and Fortinbras and his army in grey cloaks and banners came from above over a kind of battlement and dipped their flags at the final curtain.

Forbes-Robertson died sitting on the throne with the King's crown set on his lap, and was then borne off on locked shields. Leslie Howard, also, I believe, was carried off in a great procession to end the play. The poisoning of the Queen is difficult to manage, and Mr Granville-Barker has a fine idea that she should really play her death scene on the ground like the pictures of the death of Queen Elizabeth, suffering and moaning in her ladies' arms, and not dead until Hamlet says, 'Wretched queen, adieu!' I had never noticed what he so brilliantly points out – that the King, being a professional poisoner, was unable to resist using the device a second time, as so many great criminals have done. It is indeed ironic for Hamlet to realise at this moment that his mother has died just as his father did, and undoubtedly the King should have poison in a ring and the audience should see him pour it into the cup. In Tyrone Guthrie's production the scene was produced for violent melodrama, and the Queen fell from a six-foot platform into the arms of the attendants.

The supers in the scene are an added problem, for one cannot give them actions which appear violent enough to express their horror at these tragic happenings without distracting from the main characters and the dialogue and action of the scene that follows. In London I had soldiers holding the people back, but in New York the courtiers left the stage altogether just before the King was killed. There is reason, however, to keep them on the stage in order that they should be in contrast to the corpses, and so that Hamlet may have someone to whom to address his 'You that look pale and tremble at this chance'. I should like, another time, to use the old councillors and ladies-in-waiting of whom I spoke in the play scene, for it would give point to Hamlet's lines if he could indicate this group of important people in the kingdom as those to whom Horatio would afterwards justify all that Hamlet has done.

Mr McClintic invented for me the device of standing until the very end. I have never seen this done by anyone in the part and rebelled against trying it at first. It proved an admirable departure from tradition, for there are three recumbent figures on the stage already, and Hamlet in Horatio's arms is always faintly reminiscent of 'Kiss me, Hardy', at the death of Nelson. The standing figure holds the audience's attention just as they are on the verge of reaching for their hats, and 'The rest is silence'; spoken standing, appears to gain greater simplicity and significance if the actor can still command the audience with his full height, just before he falls.

To sum up these notes, I would like to say this: I have been fortunate enough to make some success and reputation in this wonderful part, and I have played it many more times in succession than I should have wished, to do anything like justice to the enormous complexity and the physical demands of the role. You will see that my mind has been torn in studying the part between a desire to walk in the traditions of the great ones and to carve out some interpretation that I might justly call my own. The result has only satisfied me very spasmodically, and I think perhaps the only really original contribution that I have made to the history of the part has been to play it successfully when I was younger than most Hamlets have been. However, I do not believe that in this realistic age we are likely to see many more Hamlets played by men of forty or fifty years of age. At least I certainly hope devoutly that I shall not be one of them. There are many parts for older men in Shakespeare, and I do not think that Hamlet is among them.

It is curious that when I first played the part in 1929 I was supposed to have given my best reading and to have been a very modern Hamlet. Now that I have studied it for eight years, people have begun to say that I am a Hamlet in the classical tradition, and I am not sure whether to take this as a compliment or not. I think it unlikely that I shall play the part again, and that is why I have attempted in these notes to describe some of the problems and questions that have occurred to me during fifteen years of reading, seeing, and thinking about the play. Few actors have time or training to be serious academic students as well, and their interest is as much in practical theatrical usage as in the research of scholars, though I suppose a great director should be a great scholar and a fine actor as well. If only Mr Granville-Barker would answer the prayers of us who love the theatre, and, instead of writing his brilliant treatises from far away, would come and work with us at the practical task of presenting Shakespeare in London and New York as he alone knows how it should be presented!

We have not many directors or actors with a strong bent for Shakespeare, and even with those who have talent there is always the danger that too much work in Shakespeare may develop a bad acting tradition and defeat its own ends. If the modern generation in the theatre is to give its best in Shakespeare it must alternate performances of classics with performances of the best modern authors and the masterpieces of Chekhov, Ibsen, Congreve, Shaw. And, above all, a really fine performance of Shakespeare demands more than a bare three weeks' rehearsal. The cast needs a fortnight's work in the speaking alone, and beyond the rehearsals of the actors there is all the preparatory work for the director, designer, musician, and stage-managers. Much of this can be roughly thought out beforehand, but how much better it could be if the play had time to grow at rehearsals, if costumes were planned for the actors who were to wear them, and the 'business' of scenes discussed, developed, and finally arranged as they grew naturally from the actor's needs. English actors resent long rehearsals. Six weeks might induce them to become inventive and creative from very boredom. The director could study them, work with them, discuss with them, not merely impose his personality and order them about like sheep – and both would gain by natural contact and familiarity. This, I am sure, is one of the secrets of companies like that of the Moscow Art Theatre and some of the famous Continental repertory companies. The plays must be cast with as much care, particularly in the smaller parts, as if they were the work of a distinguished modern author, and the director must describe and discuss his attitude towards the play with the whole cast before beginning work on it. These councils of perfection are obvious, I suppose, to any intelligent person, but it is surprising how seldom they are carried out in the theatre. *Hamlet* is nearly always a success, but shall we ever see a really perfect production of it played, not more than three times a week, as the chief glory of a theatre's repertoire?

APPENDIX III

Harley Granville-Barker on King Lear

After the death of Granville-Barker in 1946 I searched in vain for my rehearsal copy of *King Lear* in which I had hastily scribbled many of his hints on tone, motives and technical delivery of lines. Shortly before beginning to study the play again for Stratford-on-Avon in 1950, I was lucky enough to find the missing copy in a neglected corner of a drawer. Here are the majority of the notes. I add them in the hope that they may bring to others (as they do so vividly to me) an echo of the exactness which Granville-Barker showed in his criticism and guidance, and his understanding of every mood and nuance in the part of Lear. Here are the notes exactly as I scribbled them down at the time.[1]

ACT I. SCENE I

> [Lear enters ceremoniously from the side carrying a huge staff which he uses to walk with. Reaching the centre of the stage, on his way to the throne, which commands the stage up centre, he suddenly stops, and striking the staff impatiently on the floor, raps out his first command to Gloucester – then he gives the staff to an attendant and mounts the throne. Pleased. Happy.]

1 These notes were recorded by Sir John in his copy of the play – an edition now no longer available. The line numbers here given refer to Professor Sisson's edition of *The Complete Works of William Shakespeare* (Odhams, London 1954). There are slight differences between the edition used by Granville-Barker and Professor Sisson's, but it was thought advantageous to leave the line as studied by the actor.

Line

102 *Nothing will come of nothing*. First note of danger.

106 *How now, Cordelia, mend your speech a little*. Grind. Intimidation.

124 *By the sacred radiance of the sun*. Big without ponging [actor's slang for hamming].

131–2 *The barbarous Scythian*. Oath over, sulk over this. Descending passage.

139 *I loved her most*. Justify himself.

152 *With reservation of an hundred knights*. He thinks this disposes of the whole thing, lean back, happy as at opening.

178 *Kent, on thy life, no more*. Dead quiet. Turn. Stare at him.

197 *Since thou hast sought to make us break our vow*. Everyone must listen. Write this down.

205 *If on the tenth day following*. Get a note of this [to secretary]. [After exit of Kent.]
Lear – complete change – smooth, courtly, charming, anger vanished.
[To Burgundy.] Irony, smooth, cruel about Cordelia, urbanity, very ironic, schoolmaster showing up dunce.
[To France (whom he liked).] More respect, genuine. Don't look at Cordelia again.

289 *Nothing. I have sworn, I am firm*. Real, sulky. Big Ben striking. Pass by exit, cut her dead.

515 *The jewels of our father with washed eyes*. Cordelia weeps *not* for the behaviour of Lear, but because of the kindness of France in accepting her.

ACT I. SCENE IV

[With Kent in disguise. Robust, jolly, give and take, enjoy sparring. Sing, genial, throw things about (gloves, whip, etc.). Boots off, shoes on, nuisance. Suddenly checked by the insolence of the knight, continue gloves, etc., mechanically, sudden stop.]

Line

68 *Thou but rememberest me of mine own conception.* I saw it, felt it, can't be really so.

85 *Do you bandy looks with me?* Take cloth from table, strike him across the face. Stand quite still, hands on hips. Terrific. Kent trips Oswald. Roars with laughter.
[At entrance of Fool.] Sit him by me, give him food. Immensely fond, sweet to him. Eat and drink heartily. Show him off to Kent.

112 *Take heed sirrah, the whip.* Not too fast. Encourage Fool to go on, buy it. This will be a good one I expect.
No Welcome from Goneril. Suddenly notices her. Take it in.

225 *Are you our daughter?* Blank.

232 *Does any here know me?* Danger – end of careless exterior. Gasps. Feeling. Speech nothing.

243 *Your name, fair gentlewoman.* Bite. During her speech store it up – hold back.

262 *Darkness and Devils.* Crash. Pause between sentences.
[Entrance of Albany.] More Reason. Down towards her. See her. Find it.

285 *Oh, Lear, Lear, Lear.* Let go. The curse sudden, surprise the audience.
Speak nicely to Albany, going, then down to her. Strange, not loud. Deadly. Ride it.

304 *Sharper than a serpent's tooth.* Climax. Move backwards from her.

305 *Away, away.* Will not go back on it. Slow exit
[Sudden reappearance.] Broken speech in contrast to former scene. Change after 'What's the matter sir?' See Goneril. Burst into tears. Not too much. Not repeat the curse.

ACT I. SCENE V

[Represents the journey from Goneril's castle to Gloster's.]
[At entrance.] Touch of the ruler. Characteristic. Quick, not thinking of what he says. Walks continually to and fro. Stop suddenly – deep walk *I did her wrong* stop again.

Line

33/4 *Be my horses ready*? Shout. Move about.
38 *Because they are not eight*? Angry. Heard it before.
40 *Monster ingratitude*. Walk again.
43 *How's that*? Sudden.
46 *O let me not be mad*. Now afraid *inside*. Simple.
50 *Come boy*. Sustained exit. Use Fool as focal point in the scene throughout.

ACT II. SCENE IV

[Arrival at Gloster's Castle.] Pace at which you left. Start again.
[At entrance.] Puzzled but confident.

7 *Ha*? Turn. Very slow, very outraged.
15 *What's he that hath so much thy place mistook*? Deadly.
Exchange with Kent in the stocks. Pride hurt. Superb.
25 *Thou durst not do it*. Slow rhythm. Dignity offended. Too indignant to be angry.
[During Kent's speech.] Absorb the insult.
118/9 *My breath and blood*. Recover, then hysteria again.
123 *We are not ourselves*. (As he felt just now himself.)
128 *Death on my state*. Sudden rage.
133 *Duke and's wife*. More than temper.
136 *I'll beat the drum*. Deepest round this point.
139 *O me, my heart*. Physical. Entirely new voice. Quick.
Then stand still. Pay no attention to the Fool. Closed eyes, hand to head.
Entrance of Cornwall and Regan. Begin right down.
145 *Good morrow to you both*. No greeting. Cold.
147 *I am glad to see your highness*. Don't notice this.
148 *Regan I think you are*. Tender, just. (In his heart he knows.)
156/7 *Thou'lt not believe with how depraved a quality*. Literal.
161 *Say how is that*? Stern, suspicious.
167 *My curses on her*. Then control it.
182 *Never, Regan*. Definite. Then a bit petty and distracted, not deliberate.

Line

190 *You nimble lightnings*. Rash mood. Burble.

196 *No Regan thou shalt never have my curse*. Exhausted by the rage. Tender silly.

200 *'Tis not in thee*. Fear that he may be wrong. (You didn't mean it, did you?)
[Does not take in Goneril's arrival till her appearance, turns to door, and sees her suddenly. Then sees Kent too again.]

210 *Who put my man i' the stocks*? King.

221 *Who comes here? O heavens*. Knowledge gradually growing, more moved than ever.

222 *If you do love old men*? Noble, becoming helpless.

228 *O Regan, wilt thou take her by the hand*? Dignity. Slow.

237 *You! Did you*? Utter Contempt. Period.

249 *The hot-blooded France that dowerless took our youngest born*. Paint it, then off again.

253 *Slave and sumpter*. Preposterous.

256 *I prithee daughter do not make me mad*. Physical. Real. Turn swift.

260 *Or rather a disease that's in my flesh*. Rash mood. Then suffer in the head.

292 *I gave you all*. Very big. To the front. Bewildered. Not as fast as their speeches.

299 *These wicked creatures yet do look well-favour'd*. (Goneril better than Regan.) Tremble.

310 *O reason not the need*. Drop it right down. Ironic feeling. Dignity.

320 *You see me here, you gods*. Sink on to bench. Simple. Crouching attitude.

326 *Stain my man's cheeks*. Collapse here. Rash mood suddenly. Human, broken old man, futile. Suddenly looks at them. Wipe eyes. Then up and totter off but more firmly at the end for the horses.
Self-devouring rages. Physical symptoms which he ignores.

ACT III. SCENE II [*1st Storm Scene*]

Tune in. Pitch voice. Low key. Oratorio. Every word impersonal.

Line

21 *Here I stand, your slave*. Simpler. Voice down, then up. Keep still. Feet.

54 *Let the great gods*. Full value. Point to the audience.

66/7 *I am a man more sinn'd against than sinning*. Simple. Clasp head.

[GOING MAD]

86 *My wits begin to turn*. Real not pitiful.

89 *Where is this straw my fellow*. Kind, next lines casual, make little of them.
Listen tenderly to the Fool, cloak round him (*how nicely you sing*). Hold on to the edge of security. Leave stage on a high, unfinished note.

ACT III. SCENE IV [*2nd Heath scene*]

MAD now. Strange Walk. Strange Voice. Living in purely metaphysical world. At entrance. Distant, dignified.

17 *The tempest in my mind*. Point to head. Move away from them all. Words tumbling out.

24 *O Regan, Goneril*. Climax. See it all in a circle. Vision.

27 *O, that way madness lies*. Horror. Then drop it.

30 *Prithee, go in thyself*. Kind. Stoop to touch the Fool.

34 *I'll pray (and when I have prayed) then I'll sleep*. Away to thought. Kneel in mire. Hands folded conventionally.
The Fool's scream turns him off his head. Leans back on knees. Look through cage – fingers in front of face.

57 *Didst thou give all to thy daughter*. Is that all? Face each other. Still.

72 *Have his daughters brought him to this pass*. Sad dignity. Pity now new.

78 *Now all the plagues*. Just *too* dignified. (Explain to me.)

87 *Judicious punishment*. (Quite Right.)

97 *What has thou been*? Too interested. Listen to his answer and nod approval.

Line

115 *Why thou wert better in thy grave.* Speak to no one. Full value. Now faster.

123 *Off you lendings.* Rash mood suddenly back. Afterward slow, still, stare vacantly.

139 *How fares your grace?* Curious silence.
After Gloster enters. Still Important. King. Walk round stage with Edgar talking to him.

171 *First let me talk with this philosopher.* Wave Gloster aside. Keep step with Edgar.
Fantastic bowing and pantomime.

199 *Come, let's in all.* Still grand.

207 *Come, good Athenian.* Very courteous. Get him again by the arm. At the end of the scene, nod in approval, march off in same rhythm as we walked before.

ACT III. SCENE VI [*Hovel*]

Very odd and mysterious. Gradual disintegration.

11 *A King. A King.* Indignant.

20 *It shall be done.* Action does not begin till here. Firm. Sudden move. Swinging stool in hand.

31 *The foul fiend haunts poor Tom.* Stand aghast. Lunatic for the first time. Paler and paler in voice.

37 *I'll see their trial first.* Stop them dancing.

40 *You are o' the commission.* Bow, conduct him to place. He is counsel for the prosecution.

53 *She cannot deny it.* Very reasonable.

60 *Why hast thou let her 'scape?* Tiny, trembling, old man, child-like, tottering about.

66 *The little dogs and all.* Piteous. In Kent's arms. Equal value to real and imagined characters, whole scene QUIET.

84/5 *You, sir, I entertain for one of my hundred.* Exhausted courtesy to Edgar.
Sink onto bench. Lie down. Poke head out again between imaginary curtains. Then lie again hand under cheek.

ACT IV. SCENE VI [*Dover Cliff*]

Happy King of Nature. No troubles. Tremendously dignified. Branch in hand, like staff in opening scene, walk with it.

Line

113 *Give the word*. Nice. Applaud Edgar as he says 'Pass'.
117 *Ha! Goneril with a white beard*. Frightful pain. Rub head.
125 *Go to, they are not men o' their word*. Sad. All away from the others but don't move about.
130 *Ay, every inch a King*. Direct answer, change from sad mood.
134 *Die for adultery? No*. Light.
137 *Let Copulation thrive*. Almost jolly. Swing staff above head.
137 *For Gloster's bastard son*. Special.
141 *To't Luxury, pell mell*. Comedy.
142 *Behold yond simpering dame*. Horrid.
146 *The fitchew nor the soiled horse*. Words.
148 *Down from the waist*. Intimate. Quicker. Build speech.
159 *Let me wipe it first*. Real. Physical. Comfortable with Gloster.
163 *Do thy worst blind Cupid*. Coy.
Then different key, tone, pace.
169 *Read*. Very cross.
172/3 *Your eyes are in a heavy case*. Joke.
186 *Thou rascal Beadle*. Vision. Begin to get excited. Quicker. Bursts of feeling. Flow on.
199 *Get thee glass eyes*. A bit impatient with him.
After boots are off, sudden relief. Recognize Gloster slowly, comforting him (*I will preach to thee*).
212 *When we are born*. Serio-comic.
213 *This, a good block*. Very light.
217 *Kill, kill*. Build to revenge. End of scene for feeling.
220 *No rescue what! A prisoner*? Panic. Then light, helpless.
226 *This would make a man a man of salt*. Empty chatter.

ACT IV. SCENE VII [*Awakening*]

Sit in profile in chair. Hands in lap. Make them up again.

Line

55 *You do me wrong*. A bit sulky.
60 *You are a spirit I know*. Puzzled.
62 *Where have I been*? Real. Don't anticipate.
64 *I should even die with pity*. A bit cross.
68/69 *Would I were assured of my condition*. Troubled. Keep it up. Not conscious of surroundings.
87 *Be your tears wet*? Lift her head.

He hears the voice he knows, but fears so terribly she may not be Cordelia.

95 *Do not abuse me*. Strong.
102 *You must bear with me*. Cheerful. End. Come off it. Rise as if from throne. Soft dignity at exit.

ACT V. SCENE III [*Going to prison*]

10 *Come let's away to prison*. Delighted. Really happy. Dance the whole speech like a polka. Music up and down. Variety. Exit hand in hand with her, triumphant.

ACT V. SCENE III [*Death*]

308 *Howl, howl*. Take time. Dreadful.
308 *O you are men of stone*. Anger. Hold them off.
328 *Prithee away*. Strong.
331 *I killed the slave*. (You know.)
334 *I have seen the day*. Jolly. Stand firm above her body.
336 *I am old now*. Sudden break.
Forget Cordelia in passage with Kent.
345/6 *He's dead and rotten*. Suddenly sad.
351 *You are welcome hither*. Careless. Shake hands. Move away. Wander about at back of stage.
Find the body again. The rope round her neck.
Crouch by her. Kneel.
375 *Pray you, undo this button*. Real, then a cry.
376 *Look on her*. Joy.

Letters from Granville-Barker to John Gielgud on King Lear

The Athenaeum,
Pall Mall, S.W.I.

Sunday morning
[April 14, 1940]

My dear Gielgud. Lear is in your grasp.

Forget all the things I have bothered you about. Let your own now well self-disciplined instincts carry you along, and up; simply allowing the checks and changes to prevent your being carried *away.* And I prophesy – happily – great things for you.

Yrs.
H.G.B.

May 6th 1940
18 Place des États-Unis.

My dear Gielgud. Your letter of the 2nd arrived this morning. I'll take thought and answer it tomorrow.

Meanwhile here's a trifling point:

In the last scene Lear quite ignores (as you now do) the 'Tis noble Kent, your friend' and merely gives a general answer 'A plague upon you, murderers, traitors all.' And later when he looks at him and says, 'Are you not Kent?' it should clearly be in a highly indignant 'how-dare-you-enter-our-presence-after-I-have-banished-you' tone. And when Kent answers 'The same, your servant Kent' before he can go on to the rest of the line, the old gentleman should repeat, rather feebly, the magnificent 'out of my sight' gesture with which in the first scene he banished him. *'He's* a good fellow – *He'll* strike . . .' clearly refers to the Caius impersonation and the tripping up and beating of Oswald. Perhaps we did work this out.

Yrs.
H.G.B.

April 29, [1940]
18, Place des États-Unis.

My dear Gielgud. Did we ever agree as to the precise moment at which Lear goes off his head?

I believe that Poor Tom's appearance from the hovel marks it. The 'grumbling' inside, the Fool's scream of terror, the wild figure suddenly appearing – that combination would be enough to send him over the border-line. Do you mark the moment by doing something quite *new*? Difficult, I know, to find anything new to do at that moment. But something queer and significant of madness, followed (it would help) by a dead silence, before you say (again in a voice you have not used before)

Didst thou give all . . .

I don't doubt you have devised something. But thinking over the scene this struck me – ought to have struck me before; perhaps we *did* agree to it – so I drop you this line.

You're having an interesting, if exhausting, time, I am sure, and I fancy a successful one. Congratulations.

Yrs.
H.G.B.

From H. Granville-Barker
To John Gielgud

April 30, morning.
I think I have it:-
see next sheet.

. . . *shows the heavens most just.*

Lear remains on knees at end of prayer, head buried in hands.

Edg: *Father . . . poor Tom.*

make much of this; don't hurry it;
give it a 'Banshee' effect, lilt and
rhythm.

> At the sound Lear lifts his head. Face
> seen through his outspread
> fingers (suggestion of madness
> looking through bars).
> The Fool screams and runs on:
> business as at present.
> This gets Lear to his feet. He turns
> towards the hovel watching intently
> for what will emerge.

Dialogue as at present.

> Edgar's entrance and speech:
> *Away . . . warm thee,* much as
> now. And Lear immensely struck by
> it. cf.
> Hamlet-Ghost. Just as it is finishing.
> (Edg. not to hurry it) stalk him to
> present position for *Didst thou . . .*

and, as he turns for the speech, at B, we see that he is now quite off his head.

N.B. Once Edgar is on, he Kent and Fool must keep deadly still so that these movements of Lear may have their effect. Translate the Hamlet-Ghost business into terms of Lear and it will about give you the effect.

I believe this may be right. Worth trying anyhow.

APPENDIX IV

Shakespeare Plays Directed by John Gielgud

The Merchant of Venice	(1932)	The Old Vic, London. Peggy Ashcroft, Malcolm Keen.
	(1938)	Queen's Theatre, London. Peggy Ashcroft, John Gielgud.
Hamlet	(1934)	New Theatre, London. Laura Cowie, Jessica Tandy, Frank Vosper, John Gielgud.
	(1939)	Lyceum Theatre, London. Fay Compton, Laura Cowie, Jack Hawkins, John Gielgud.
Romeo and Juliet	(1932)	The OUDS, Oxford. Edith Evans, Peggy Ashcroft.
	(1935)	New Theatre, London. Edith Evans, Peggy Ashcroft. Laurence Olivier and John Gielgud alternated in the parts of Romeo and Mercutio.
Macbeth	(1942)	Piccadilly Theatre, London. Gwen Ffrangcon-Davies, John Gielgud.
	(1952)	Memorial Theatre, Stratford-on-Avon. Margaret Leighton, Ralph Richardson.
Much Ado About Nothing	(1949)	Memorial Theatre, Stratford-on-Avon. Diana Wynyard, Anthony Quayle.

	(1950)	Memorial Theatre, Stratford-on-Avon. Peggy Ashcroft, John Gielgud.
	(1952)	Phoenix Theatre, London. Diana Wynyard, John Gielgud.
	(1955)	Palace Theatre, London. Peggy Ashcroft, John Gielgud.
	(1959)	New York, USA Margaret Leighton, John Gielgud.
Twelfth Night	(1955)	Memorial Theatre, Stratford-on-Avon. Vivien Leigh, Laurence Olivier.
King Lear	(1950)	Memorial Theatre, Stratford-on-Avon. Peggy Ashcroft, John Gielgud. (co-director: Anthony Quayle)

APPENDIX V

ROMEO AND JULIET

RADA Theatre
1924
Directed by Eric Bush

Escalus, Prince of Verona	Denis Watson
Paris	John Gielgud
Montague	Robert Speaight
Capulet	G. Gravely Edwards
Old Capulet	Timothy Speaight
Romeo	Gyles Isham
Mercutio	Eric Bush
Benvolio	Cecil Bellamy
Tybalt	Rodney Hannen
Friar Lawrence	Basil Maine
Friar John	Norman Prince
Balthazar	Cecil Bellamy
Sampson	Josselyn Hennessey
Peter	H. Wilson Wiley
Abraham	Leigh Ashton
An Apothecary	Robert Speaight
Page to Paris	Ailsey Lazarus
Lady Montague	Muriel Deason
Lady Capulet	Virginia Isham
Juliet	Paulise de Bush
Nurse to Juliet	Margaret Calthrop
Chorus	Joan Buckmaster

Maskers:
Phyllis Buckland, Enid Forsdick, Richard Cooper,
Norman Prince

HENRY IV (PART I)

The Old Vic
1930
Directed by Harcourt Williams

King Henry IV	Alfred Sangster
Earl of Westmoreland	Wilfrid Grantham
Sir Walter Blunt	Peter Taylor-Smith
John of Lancaster	Anthony Hawtrey
Sir John Falstaff	Henry Wolston
Henry, Prince of Wales	Ralph Richardson
Poins	Leslie French
Thomas Percy, Earl of Worcester	George Howe
Henry Percy, Earl of Northumberland	Valentine Dyall
Henry Percy, surnamed Hotspur	John Gielgud
1st Carrier	Farquharson Small
2nd Carrier	Leslie Young
Gadshill	Eric Phillips
A Chamberlain	Victor Peduzzi
Bardolph	Francis Curtler
Peto	Clephan Bell
1st Traveller	Philip Fothergill
2nd Traveller	David Balfour
Lady Percy	Dorothy Green
Francis	Gordon Richardson
A Vintner	Lyon Brown
Mistress Quickly	Elsa Palmer
A Sheriff	Peter Taylor-Smith
Owen Glendower	Powell Lloyd
Edmund Mortimer, Earl of March	Richard Riddle
Lady Mortimer	Doreen Purdy
Archibald, Earl of Douglas	Valentine Dyall
A Messenger	James Lytton
Sir Richard Vernon	Eric Phillips
The Archbishop of York	Owen P. Smyth
Sir Michael, his friend	Harold Chapin

KING LEAR

The Old Vic
1931
Directed by Harcourt Williams

Earl of Kent	Ralph Richardson
Earl of Gloucester	George Howe
Edmund, bastard son to Gloucester	Robert Speaight
Lear, King of Britain	John Gielgud
Goneril	Dorothy Green
Regan	Elsa Palmer
Cordelia	Patricia MacNabb
Duke of Albany	Henry Wolston
Duke of Cornwall	Alfred Sangster
Duke of Burgundy	Wilfrid Grantham
King of France	Anthony Hawtrey
Edgar, son to Gloucester	Eric Portman
Oswald, steward to Goneril	Eric Phillips
Fool	Leslie French
Curan	Gordon Richardson
A Gentleman	Valentine Dyall
A Servant to Cornwall	Peter Taylor-Smith
2nd Servant	Wilfrid Grantham
3rd Servant	Richard Riddle
Old Man, tenant to Gloucester	Farquharson Small
A Doctor	Peter Taylor-Smith
A Herald	James Lytton
A Messenger	David Balfour

Knights, ladies, messengers and attendants:
Phillip Fothergill, Harold Chapin, Clephan Bell,
Lyon Brown, Frances Brady, Doreen Purdy,
Pamela Henry-May, Doreen Barrington,
Mary Dumphreys, Ethel Glendinning,
Phyllis Homfray, Prudence Magor,
Ursula Martindale, Christian Malvery
Costumes and settings
designed and arranged by Owen P. Smyth

HAMLET

New Theatre
1934
Directed by John Gielgud

Bernardo	George Devine
Francisco	Peter Murray-Hill
Horatio	Jack Hawkins
Marcellus	Howieson Culff
Ghost of Hamlet's Father	William Devlin
Claudius, King of Denmark	Frank Vosper
Laertes	Glen Byam Shaw
Polonius	George Howe
Hamlet, Prince of Denmark	John Gielgud
Gertrude, Queen of Denmark	Laura Cowie
Ophelia	Jessica Tandy
Reynaldo	Cecil Winter
Rosencrantz	Richard Ainley
Guildenstern	Anthony Quayle
1st Player	George Devine
2nd Player	Sam Beazley
3rd Player	Alec Guinness
4th Player	Ian Atkins
5th Player	Richard Dare
Norwegian Captain	Peter Murray-Hill
Fortinbras, Prince of Norway	Geoffrey Toone
A Courtier	Frith Banbury
1st Grave Digger	Ben Field
2nd Grave Digger	Lyon Playfair
Priest	Cecil Winter
Osric	Alec Guinness

Court Ladies:
Jean Winstanley, Ethel Glendinning,
Hermione Hannen, Doris Johnstone
Courtiers, ruffians, etc:
John Brown, Philip Clowes, Cedric Bowden,
Peter Trent, Ian Atkins, Richard Dare, Guy Vivian
Scenery and costumes by Motley

RICHARD II

Queen's Theatre
1937
Directed by John Gielgud

Richard II	John Gielgud
John of Gaunt	Leon Quartermaine
Henry Bolingbroke	Michael Redgrave
Thomas Mowbray	Glen Byam Shaw
Duchess of Gloucester	Dorothy Green
Duke of Surrey, Lord Marshal	Anthony Quayle
Duke of Aumerle	Alec Guinness
Herald to Bolingbroke	Alastair Bannerman
Herald to Mowbray	Denis Carew
Green	Dennis Price
Bushey	Harry Andrews
Edmund of Langley, Duke of York	George Howe
Queen to King Richard	Peggy Ashcroft
Earl of Northumberland	Frederick Lloyd
Lord Ross	Ernest Hare
Lord Willoughby	Hereward Russell
Bagot	Pardoe Woodman
Henry Percy	John Ford
Lord Berkeley	Alastair Bannerman
Captain of a band of Welshmen	Anthony Quayle
The Earl of Salisbury	Ernest Hare
Bishop of Carlisle	Harcourt Williams
Sir Stephen Scroop	Glen Byam Shaw
A Lady attending on the Queen	Merula Salaman
A Gardener	George Devine
Lord Fitzwater	Harry Andrews
Duchess of York	Barbara Dillon
Sir Pierce of Exton	Harry Andrews
Servant to Exton	Dennis Price
A Groom of the Stable	Alec Guiness
Gaoler	Ernest Hare

Designs by Motley

KING LEAR

The Old Vic
1940
Directed by Lewis Casson
and Harley Granville-Barker

Earl of Kent	Lewis Casson
Earl of Gloucester	Nicholas Hannen
Edmund, bastard son to Gloucester	Jack Hawkins
Lear, King of Britain	John Gielgud
Goneril	Cathleen Nesbitt
Cordelia	Jessica Tandy
Regan	Fay Compton
Duke of Albany	Harcourt Williams
Duke of Cornwall	Andrew Cruickshank
Duke of Burgundy	Basil Coleman
King of France	Alan MacNaughtan
Edgar, son to Gloucester	Robert Harris
Oswald, steward to Goneril	Julian Somers
A Knight	Frank Tickle
Fool	Stephen Haggard
Curan	Charles Staite
A Gentleman	Frank Tickle
1st Servant to Cornwall	John McCallum
2nd Servant	Alan MacNaughtan
3rd Servant	James Donald
Old Man, tenant to Gloucester	Frank Tickle
Doctor	Charles Staite
1st Gentleman Attendant on Cordelia	Basil Coleman
2nd Gentleman Attendant on Cordelia	Laurence Payne
Captain, employed by Edmund	James Donald
Herald	John McCallum

Scenery and costumes by Roger Furse
Music arranged by Herbert Menges

MACBETH

On Tour and at the Piccadilly Theatre
1942
Directed by John Gielgud

Duncan, King of Scotland	Nicholas Hannen
Malcolm	Emrys Jones
Donalbain	John Shepherd
Macbeth	John Gielgud
Banquo	Leon Quartermaine
Macduff	Francis Lister
Lennox	Alan Badel
Ross	Abraham Sofaer
Menteith	George Woodbridge
Angus	Frank Thornton
Caithness	Frederick Annerley
Fleance, son to Banquo	Michael Gainsborough
Siward, Earl of Northumberland	Leon Quartermaine
Young Siward	John Shepherd
Seyton	Charles Maunsell
Boy, son to Macduff	David Baxter
A Scottish Doctor	A. Bromley-Davenport
A Porter	George Woodbridge
First Murderer	Tarver Penna
Second Murderer	Charles Maunsell
Third Murderer	Robert Griffith
Servant to Macduff	Alan Badel
Messenger to Lady Macduff	Robert Griffith
Lady Macbeth	Gwen Ffrangcon-Davies
Lady Macduff	Thea Holme
Gentlewoman	Frances Ruttledge

The Weird Sisters
Ernest Thesiger, Annie Esmond, Dorothy Green
Decor by Michael Ayrton and John Minton
Costumes by Michael Ayrton
Incidental music composed by William Walton

HAMLET

Theatre Royal Haymarket
1944
Directed by George Rylands

Claudius, King of Denmark	Leslie Banks
Hamlet, Prince of Denmark	John Gielgud
Polonius	Miles Malleson
Horatio	Francis Lister
Laertes	Patrick Crean
Voltimand	Ernest Hare
Cornelius	Darcy Conyers
Rosencrantz	Max Adrian
Guildenstern	John Blatchley
Osric	Max Adrian
Captain of Fortinbras' Army	Ernest Hare
A Gentleman	Donald Bain
A Priest	Francis Drake
Marcellus	Cecil Trouncer
Bernardo	George Woodbridge
Francisco	Ernest Hare
Reynaldo	D.J. Williams
Ghost of Hamlet's Father	Leon Quartermaine
Player King	Cecil Trouncer
Player Queen	Eric Goldie
3rd Player	Tom Colmer
4th Player	D.J. Williams
1st Gravedigger	George Woodbridge
2nd Gravedigger	John Blatchley
Fortinbras, Prince of Norway	Tom Colmer
Gertrude, Queen of Denmark	Marian Spencer
Ophelia	Peggy Ashcroft

Setting by Ruth Keating
Costumes designed by Jeanetta Cochrane
The Play lit by Hamish Wilson
Music composed and arranged by Leslie Bridgewater

MUCH ADO ABOUT NOTHING

Shakespeare Memorial Theatre
1950
Directed by John Gielgud

Don Pedro, Prince of Arragon	Leon Quartermaine
Don John	Alan Badel
Claudio	Eric Lander
Benedick	John Gielgud
Leonato, Governor of Messina	Andrew Cruickshank
Antonio	Harold Kasket
Balthazar	John York
Borachio	Paul Hardwick
Conrade	Robert Shaw
Dogberry, a Constable	George Rose
Verges, a Headborough	Richard Dare
Friar Francis	Robert Hardy
A Sexton	Ronald Hines
A Boy	John Wright
Messenger	Nigel Green
First Watch	Percy Herbert
Second Watch	Charles Lepper
Third Watch	Hugh Dunbar
Hero	Barbara Jefford
Beatrice	Peggy Ashcroft
Margaret	Mairhi Russell
Ursula	Maxine Audley

Scenery and costumes by Mariano Andreu
Incidental music by Leslie Bridgewater
Dances arranged by Pauline Grant
Lighting by Christopher West

JULIUS CAESAR

Shakespeare Memorial Theatre
1950
Directed by Anthony Quayle and Michael Langham

Julius Caesar	Andrew Cruickshank
Octavius Caesar	Alan Badel
Marcus Antonius	Anthony Quayle
M. Æmil. Lepidus	Cyril Conway
Cicero	Richard Dare
Marcus Brutus	Harry Andrews
Cassius	John Gielgud
Casca	Michael Gwynn
Trebonius	John Money
Ligarius	Geoffrey Bayldon
Decius Brutus	Nigel Green
Metellus Cimber	Peter Norris
Cinna	Percy Herbert
Flavius	Robert Hardy
A Cobbler	Michael Bates
Lucius	Eric Lander
Artemidorus of Cnidos	John Gay
A Soothsayer	Timothy Bateson
A Messenger	Robert Shaw
An Officer	Ronald Hines
Cinna, a poet	Harold Kasket
Lucilius	John Dunbar
Titinius	Nigel Green
Messala	Paul Hardwick
Clitus	Cyril Conway
Claudius	Godfrey Bond
Strato	Michael Kelly
Dardanius	Robert Hardy
Pindarus	John Gay
Calpurnia	Barbara Jefford
Portia	Gwen Ffrangcon-Davies

Scenery and costumes by Warwick Armstrong
Incidental music by Leslie Bridgewater

MEASURE FOR MEASURE

Shakespeare Memorial Theatre
1950
Directed by Peter Brook

Vincentio, the Duke	Harry Andrews
Escalus	Harold Kasket
Angelo	John Gielgud
Lucio	Leon Quartermaine
First Gentleman	Robert Hardy
Second Gentleman	Robert Shaw
Mistress Overdone	Rosalind Atkinson
Pompey	George Rose
Claudio	Alan Badel
Provost	Michael Gwynn
Friar Thomas	Cyril Conway
Isabella	Barbara Jefford
Francisca	Romany Evens
Elbow	Michael Bates
Froth	Geoffrey Bayldon
A Justice	Peter Norris
Servant to Angelo	Timothy Bateson
Juliet	Hazel Penwarden
A Boy, attendant on Mariana	Mairhi Russell
Abhorson	Nigel Green
Barnardine	Paul Hardwick
Friar Peter	Peter Norris

Citizens, soldiers, warders, prisoners:
Marjorie Steel, Felicity Barrington, Eric Lander,
Richard Dare, John Dunbar, David Lytton, John Gay,
Ronald Hines, Peter Halliday, Michael Ney,
Michael Atkinson, Ward Williams, Peter Jackson,
David Woodman, Charles Lepper, Godfrey Bond,
Edward Atienza, Michael Ferrey, John York,
John Wright
Scenery and costumes designed by Peter Brook with
Michael Northen and Kegan Smith
Music adviser: Leslie Bridgewater

KING LEAR

Shakespeare Memorial Theatre,
Stratford
1950
Directed by John Gielgud and Anthony Quayle

Lear, King of Britain	John Gielgud
Goneril	Maxine Audley
Regan	Gwen Ffrangcon-Davies
Cordelia	Peggy Ashcroft
Duke of Albany	Michael Gwynn
Duke of Cornwall	Paul Hardwick
King of France	Basil Hoskins
Duke of Burgundy	Robert Shaw
Earl of Gloucester	Leon Quartermaine
Edgar, son to Gloucester	Harry Andrews
Edmund, bastard son to Gloucester	Nigel Green
Earl of Kent	Andrew Cruickshank
Fool	Alan Badel
Oswald, steward to Goneril	George Rose
Knight, attendant to Lear	Robert Hardy
Curan	Peter Henchie
Old Man, tenant to Gloucester	Godfrey Bond
Doctor	Peter Norris
Herald	John Money
Servants to Cornwall	Geoffrey Bayldon
	Michael Bates
	Peter Halliday
A Captain, employed by Edmund	Ward Williams
A Captain, employed by Albany	Michael Kelly

Scenery and costumes by Leslie Hurry
Incidental music by Cedric Thorpe-Davie
Technical and lighting direction by Michael Northen
Music Adviser: Leslie Bridgewater

THE WINTER'S TALE

Phoenix Theatre
1951
Directed by Peter Brook

Leontes, King of Sicilia	John Gielgud
Hermione, Queen to Leontes	Diana Wynyard
Mamillius	Robert Anderson
Polixenes, King of Bohemia	Brewster Mason
Camillo	Michael Goodliffe
Emilia	Hazel Terry
Antigonus	Lewis Casson
First Lord	Hugh Stewart
Second Lord	John Moffatt
Third Lord	Kenneth Edwards
Paulina	Flora Robson
A Gaoler	John Whiting
Cleomenes	Paul Hardwick
Dion	Michael Nightingale
A Bear	Churton Fairman
A Mariner	Michael Nightingale
Old Shepherd	George Howe
Young Shepherd	Philip Guard
Time	Norman Bird
Autolycus	George Rose
Perdita	Virginia McKenna
Florizel, Prince of Bohemia	Richard Gale
Dorcas	Joy Rogers
Mopsa	Charlotte Mitchell
Paulina's steward	John Moffatt

Lords, ladies, servants,
shepherds and shepherdesses:
Denys Graham, William Patrick,
Churton Fairman, Oliver Cox, Philip Pearman,
Sarah Davies, Frances Hyland, Charles Doran,
Michael Cleveland

Scenery and costumes by Sophie Fedorovitch

THE TRAGEDY OF KING LEAR

European Tour and Palace Theatre
1955
Directed by John Gielgud and George Devine

The Earl of Kent	Anthony Nicholls
The Earl of Gloucester	George Devine
Edmund, his bastard son	Harold Lang
Lear, King of Britain	John Gielgud
Goneril	Helen Cherry
The Duke of Albany	Raymond Westwell
Regan	Moira Lister
The Duke of Cornwall	Anthony Ireland
Cordelia	Claire Bloom
The Duke of Burgundy	Paul Hardwick
The King of France	Jeremy Burnham
Edgar, elder son to Gloucester	Richard Easton
Oswald, steward to Goneril	John Garley
Knight, attending on Lear	Powys Thomas
Fool	David O'Brien
Curan	David Marlowe
Servants to Cornwall	Ken Wynne
	David Conville
	Michael Malnick
Old Man, tenant to Gloucester	Paul Hardwick
A Doctor	Peter Retey
A Soldier in Cordelia's army	Michael Spice
A Captain in Edmund's army	Michael Malnick
A Herald	Beverley Cross

Knights, servants, soldiers:
Nicholas Brady, Brian Hankins, Timothy Harley,
Gary Raymond

Scenery and costumes by Isamu Noguchi

THE TEMPEST

The Shakespeare Memorial Theatre and
Drury Lane
1957
Directed by Peter Brook

The Master of a Ship	Peter Palmer
A Boatswain	Ron Haddrick
Alonso, King of Naples	Robert Harris
Antonio, usurping Duke of Milan	Mark Dignam
Gonzalo	Cyril Luckham
Sebastian	Robin Lloyd
Adrian	Toby Robertson
Miranda	Doreen Aris
Prospero, the rightful Duke of Milan	John Gielgud
Ariel	Brian Bedford
Caliban	Alec Clunes
Ferdinand	Richard Johnson
Trinculo	Clive Revill
Stephano	Patrick Wymark
Iris	Olive Gregg
Ceres	Stephanie Bidmead
Juno	Ellen McIntosh

Mariners, nymphs, reapers and others:
Mavis Edwards, Elizabeth Evans, Pamela Taylor,
Eileen Atkins, Rex Robinson, Robert Arnold,
Thane Bettany, Antony Brown, Derek Mayhew,
John Murray Scott, Barry Warren, Edward Caddick,
Simon Carter, John Davidson, Henry Davies,
William Elmhirst, Kenneth Gilbert, Julian Glover,
John Grayson, Norman Miller, John Salway,
Gordon Souter, Roy Spencer, Gordon Wright
Designs and music by Peter Brook
with Michael Northen, Kegan Smith,
William Blezard
Choreography by Raimonda Orselli
Lighting supervision: Joe Davis

THE TEMPEST

The National Theatre at the Old Vic
1974
Directed by Peter Hall

Alonso, King of Naples	Joseph O'Conor
Sebastian	William Squire
Prospero, the rightful Duke of Milan	John Gielgud
Antonio, the usurping Duke of Milan	Cyril Cusack
Ferdinand	Rupert Frazer
Gonzalo	David Markham
Adrian	Peter Rocca
Francisco	Christopher Guard
Caliban	Denis Quilley
Trinculo	Julian Orchard
Stephano	Arthur Lowe
The Master of a ship	Alex McCrindle
Boatswain	James Mellor
Miranda	Jenny Agutter
Ariel	Michael Feast
Iris	Julie Covington
Juno	Dana Gillespie

and
Dai Bradley, Bryan Brown, Jane Carr,
David Dixon, Colin Fay, Glyn Grain,
Patti Love, Ian Mackenzie, James Mellor,
Peter Needham, Judith Paris, Veronica Quilligan,
Gerard Ryder, Keith Skinner, James Smith,
Stephen Williams
Musicians:
Chuck Mallett, Barry Mason, Laurie Morgan
Designs by John Bury
Lighting by John Bury and Leonard Tucker
Music by Gryphon
Movement by Claude Chagrin
Masks and shapes by Jennifer Carey

JULIUS CAESAR

National Theatre
1977
Directed by John Schlesinger

Julius Caesar	John Gielgud
Marcus Brutus	Brian Cox
Caius Cassius	Ronald Pickup
Casca	Gawn Grainger
Decius Brutus	Oliver Cotton
Cinna	Pitt Wilkinson
Metellus Cimber	Peter Needham
Trebonius	Michael Beint
Caius Ligarius	Norman Claridge
Mark Antony	Mark McManus
Octavius Caesar	Ian Charleson
Lepidus	Liam O'Callaghan
Flavius	Glyn Grain
Marullus	Tom Wilkinson
Cicero	Martin Friend
Publius	Peter Carlisle
Popilius Lena	John Gill
Portia	Rowena Cooper
Calpurnia	Ann Firbank
Soothsayer	Keith Skinner
Companion to Soothsayer	Edna Doré
Lucius	Paul Henley
Artemidorus	Daniel Thorndike
Cinna the poet	Andrew Hilton
Cobbler	Trevor Ray
Carpenter	Timothy Block
Officer to Caesar	Ray Edwards
Officer to Antony	Shane Connaughton
Officer to Octavius	Brian Kent

Augurers
Olu Jacobs, Stanley Lloyd, Dennis Tynsley

Lucilius	Glyn Grain

Volumnius	Andrew Hilton
Young Cato	Chris Hunter
Clitus	Peter Needham
Dardanius	Timothy Block
Messala	Oliver Cotton
Strato	Pitt Wilkinson
Varro	Jonathan Battersby
Claudius	Stanley Lloyd
Titinius	Tom Wilkinson
Pindarus	Olu Jacobs
Poet	Michael Beint

with
Shulie Bannister, Vivienne Burgess,
Imogen Claire, Irene Gorst, Marianne Morley,
Peter Rocca
Musicians:
Marcio Mattos, Leroy Cowie (double bass),
Laurie Morgan, Sean Hooper (percussion),
Andrew Mitchell, Simon Ferguson (trumpets),
Martin Nicholls (trombone),
John Wesley Barker (flute)
Designs by John Bury
Lighting by David Hersey
Music composed by Harrison Birtwistle

INDEX

SHAKESPEARE'S PLAYS IN PERFORMANCE by John Russell Brown

In this volume, John Russell Brown snatches Shakespeare from the clutches of dusty academics and thrusts him centerstage where he belongs—in performance.

Brown's thorough analysis of the theatrical experience of Shakespeare forcibly demonstrates how the text is brought to life: awakened, colored, emphasized, and extended by actors and audiences, designers and directors.

> "A knowledge of what precisely can and should happen when a play is performed is, for me, the essential first step towards an understanding of Shakespeare."
>
> —*from the Introduction by John Russell Brown*

paper•ISBN 1-55783-136-X•

SHAKESCENES: SHAKESPEARE FOR TWO

The Shakespeare Scenebook

EDITED AND WITH AN INTRODUCTION BY JOHN RUSSELL BROWN

Shakespeare's plays are not the preserve of "Shakespearean Actors" who specialize in a remote species of dramatic life. Shakespeare asks to be performed by all good actors. Here in the introduction, "Advice to Actors," and in the notes to each of thirty–five scenes, John Russell Brown offers sensible guidance for those who have little or no experience with the formidable Bard. Thirty-five scenes are presented in newly edited texts, with notes which clarify meanings, topical references, puns, ambiguities, etc. Each scene has been chosen for its independent life requiring only the simplest of stage properties and the barest of spaces. A brief description of characters and situation prefaces each scene and is followed by a commentary which discusses its major acting challenges and opportunities.

paper • ISBN 1-55783-049-5

THE ACTOR AND THE TEXT
by Cicely Berry

As voice director of the Royal Shakespeare Company, Cicely Berry has worked with actors such as Jeremy Irons, Derek Jacobi, Jonathan Pryce, Sinead Cusack and Antony Sher. *The Actor and The Text* brings Ms. Berry's methods of applying vocal production skills within a text to the general public.

While this book focuses primarily on speaking Shakespeare, Ms. Berry also includes the speaking of some modern playwrights, such as Edward Bond.

As Ms. Berry describes her own volume in the introduction:

" ... this book is not simply about making the voice sound more interesting. It is about getting inside the words we use ...It is about making the language organic, so that the words act as a spur to the sound ..."

paper•ISBN 1-155783-138-6

RECYCLING SHAKESPEARE
by Charles Marowitz

Marowitz' irreverent approach to the bard is destined to outrage Shakespearean scholars across the globe. Marowitz rejects the notion that a "classic" is a sacrosanct entity fixed in time and bounded by its text. A living classic, according to Marowitz, should provoke lively response—even indignation!

In the same way that Shakespeare himself continued to meditate and transform his own ideas and the shape they took, Marowitz gives us license to continue that meditation in productions extrapolated from Shakespeare's work. Shakespeare becomes the greatest of all catalysts who stimulates a constant reformulation of the fundamental questions of philosophy, history and meaning. Marowitz introduces us to Shakespeare as an active contemporary collaborator who strives with us to yield a vibrant contemporary theatre.

paper • ISBN: 1-55783-094-0

An Actor and His Time

JOHN GIELGUD

"FUNNY, TOUCHING, BRILLIANT, SPECIAL, THE BEST — EXACTLY LIKE JOHN GIELGUD."
— LAUREN BACALL

"A WONDERFUL BOOK . . . THE RESULT IS MAGICAL . . . GIELGUD IS THE GREATEST ACTOR OF THIS CENTURY . . . WE HAVE NO BETTER CHRONICLER OF THE THEATRE IN HIS TIME . . . AN ASTUTE OBSERVER, A SLY HUMORIST."
— SHERIDAN MORLEY, *THE LITERARY REVIEW*

"I CAN HEAR HIS SUPERB VOICE IN EVERY LINE."
— ALEC GUINNESS

"A FASCINATING ACCOUNT OF A LEGENDARY CAREER."
— *SUNDAY TELEGRAPH*

"A RARE DELIGHT — FULL OF WIT, THEATRICAL HISTORY, ANECDOTES, AND WISDOM."
— DIANA RIGG

CLOTH• ISBN 1-55783-299-4
PAPER• ISBN 1-55783-415-6